"This outstanding collection of vignettes provides the reader a fascinating glimpse of the character, strength, and challenges of the men and women who support those of us who serve in the Armed Forces. Without them, we could achieve nothing. With them, we meet the mission on many fronts, in many lands, in many ways. Their service — their sacrifices — are no less important than those who wear the uniform. Read their stories — they are truly inspirational!"

Wm. Dean Lee, VADM, USCG, (ret)

"Calling all patriots! Whether you are a military family or know one, these pages radiate the resiliency of the American spirit. These stories of military families will equip and encourage anyone to come alongside those wearing a uniform with the love of Christ. A wonderful gift and resource to help us all serve our soldiers' families well."

Erica Wiggenhorn, Bible teacher and author of *Unexplainable Jesus: Rediscovering the God You Thought You Knew* **by Moody Publishers**

"In recent years I have enveloped into my circle a group of *soul strong* women who have raised my awareness of both the sacrifice and significance of those in our armed forces. Women whose voices must be heard! That's why I'm delighted that Megan B. Brown has edited the new volume *Brave Women Strong Faith*, that we might begin to understand the lives of military women who face deployment, battle, loneliness, upheaval—all through a commitment of their family to serving our country. The beauty of this book is the stories—real life adventures of very young women who continue to dare, risk, persevere, and find God's goodness even in loss. As you sense their struggles, see their spirit, and savor their strength, may you embrace your own inner warrior to fight the battles ahead."

Lucinda Secrest McDowell, author of *Soul Strong and Life-Giving Choices*

"This must-read collection of true stories will break your heart and warm your soul. Real life for military spouses is more than flags and fireworks and shopping trips to the PX. These powerful stories of resilience, loneliness, grief, and loyalty will inspire you to be brave. To make best friends out of strangers. To flourish where you are right now. To pursue your purpose. To trust God to fill in the gaps."

Robyn Dykstra, Christian author and speaker

"*Brave Women Strong Faith* is a collection of stories every person in America should read. Learn what makes these women unique and priceless to our nation. Understand the feelings and issues experienced by thousands of women in our country. Become aware of the needs and desires of women in your community who want to connect with you, but face obstacles we "civilians" struggle to understand. This collection will help you truly see the military women around you, value what they have to offer, and hear how they can impact the lives in your community and in our nation."

Kim Erickson, author of *Surviving Sorrow: A Mother's Guide to Living with Loss* (Moody Publishers 2020) and *His Last Words: What Jesus Taught and Prayed in His Final Hours* (Moody Publishers 2017)

"The voices of these military wives are real and raw. Their stories reveal rare views of the home side of deployment few of us understand. The high cost of their service to our country goes mainly unseen. Reading this book prepares your heart to stand alongside them. Through their exhaustion of painful good-byes and constant start-overs, these bold women share their hard-learned lessons. All of us whether in the military or civilian life will grow stronger by reading what only they can offer. This book will change you deeply. Behind each sacrifice is a woman on a mission to let her world know your spiritual lifeline is within God's faith community of care and love. This is where the greatest battles are won. This book is a battle cry of praise!"

**Anne Denmark M. Ed., PCC,
Professional Certified Coach**

"You hold in your hands a treasure trove of stories—compelling, courageous, and true stories—that will touch your heart, and give you hope. How I wish this devotional book had been around in the 1960's, '70's and 80's when, as military couples often separated by an ocean and a 7-cent stamp, we would have benefitted from the perspectives and insights offered here. A new generation of brave military spouses has come together in these pages to share with you some of their life struggles: the messy and the mundane, the loneliness and woundedness; the waiting, grief, losses, fearful unknowns, and so much more. But they don't leave you there; they move you forward, to the "But God..." part of their redemptive journeys. They come alongside, with the heart of a caring sister and a loving arm around you, proclaiming what they learned, how they grew, and where you too can find hope and healing. Whether you've ever been in a military community or not, you will come away encouraged, inspired, and closer to the God who shows up in the hardships and heartaches of life, to bring you hope. This is a book you don't want to miss."

Sandi Banks, speaker, author of *Anchors of Hope*

"I had no idea what being a military spouse was supposed to look like. My husband made a commitment to serve his country and I was committed to be his partner in life. Like the women I met on these pages, military life brought great challenges that produced inner strength, personal fulfillment, deep relationships, and spiritual transformation. The stories held in this anthology are written by women I am proud to call my tribe. Theirs are stories of sisterhood, stories of commitment, and stories of resiliency. These are women who sacrifice much and ask for little. Yet, they are not martyrs; they are unsung heroes. I celebrate their stories and their lives."

Brenda C. Pace, 28-year Army Wife, speaker, author, *Journey of a Military Wife* (ABS), *The One-Year Yellow Ribbon Devotional* (Tyndale), *Medals Above My Heart* (Broadman & Holman), Advisor, Planting Roots

"Raw, Real, Relevant. Megan and her cohort of story tellers holds nothing back about the military life. These real-life stories will validate and affirm those of us associated with the military. All those who love military servicemembers and their families will be amazed and grateful for the freedoms we have because of the selfless sacrifices of the military family."

COL(R) Steve Myer and Carleene Myer, National Directors for Cru Military

"I wish *Brave Women and Strong Faith* could be distributed by military chapels to *every* military spouse. As the wife of a retired Air Force officer, I remember being given a small book by the wife of my husband's commanding officer when we first joined the service years ago, instructing me on etiquette, table setting, and other superficial things to enhance my husband's military career. However, this powerful new book is SO much more valuable and relevant. The authors, all military women and/or spouses, share honestly about often overwhelming challenges as well as the joy of serving as a team, the value of friendship, the availability of resources, and so much more.

It is also an important book for each of us as civilians to read because it will encourage us to cheer for these BRAVE WOMEN with strong faith and to pray for them! It will open our eyes to the vast opportunities these women have as ambassadors for Jesus, whether they are left behind to bravely cope and handle everything as their husbands deploy on unaccompanied duty, or as they bravely accompany them around the globe."

Jennie Afman Dimkoff, international author, speaker, storyteller

"Here in these pages lie true stories of military life. They capture the heartache, fear, loneliness, and uncertainty of this nomadic life. But even more amazing, they also capture God's faithfulness, God's goodness, and God's love. Whether you live in this military culture or not, you will find inspiration and encouragement as you seek the Lord wherever you are today."

Kori Yates, Planting Roots Director

"Last year I had the blessing of meeting several of the women who authored this poignant book. Hearing the stories of these military wives gave me a sneak peek into a new world, and immediately the first word I thought as I left my time with them was "warriors." This inspiring book written by these warriors feels like holy ground to me. They share vulnerably, openly, and allow us to enter into a world that I think it is of utmost importance for us as civilians to learn. These stories of surviving suffering, searching for community, and finding hope in the midst of the unknown can inspire and encourage us all. Everyone needs a copy of this book to find hope for ourselves in a world of uncertainty while seeing into the lives of these warriors, so we can learn how to come alongside them and champion them and their families."

Jennifer Hand, Executive Director of Coming Alive Ministries

"This book is a beautiful compilation of warrior women opening their scars to offer healing hope to the world around them. Their obedience to God's calling on their lives will challenge you to love on our military community like never before. As you turn each page, you will be compelled to link up arms in action with them to spread the good news of the Gospel."

**Caris Snider, author of *Anxiety Elephants*
*31 Day Devotional***

"*Brave Women Strong Faith* will tug at your heart with the incredible stories of loneliness, fear, dealing with pain trauma, and embracing uncertainty that are woven into the fabric of military spouses' lives. The daughter of a proud Navy veteran, I leaned into their stories, knowing that my own mom likely faced similar challenges while my dad served in the years before I was born. These stories beautifully illustrate the transforming power of friendship, community and faith that we all need to embrace as we face our own challenges in life. Lean in and be inspired. When you do, you'll understand why I consider these women warriors."

**Susan Call, author of *Searching for Purple Cows:*
*A Story of Hope***

FEATURING AUTHORS
Amanda Huffman, Kennita Williams,
Richelle Futch, Sherry Eifler

BRAVE Women, STRONG Faith

Inspiring Stories
by Military Women
and Wives

BROOKSTONE
PUBLISHING GROUP

Compilation and Collection Copyright © 2020 Megan B. Brown

All rights reserved. No part of this book may be reproduced in any form or by any electronic or mechanical means, including information storage and retrieval systems, without permission in writing from the publisher, except by reviewers, who may quote brief passages in a review.

The copyright in *Brave Women, Strong Faith*, otherwise known as the work, is independent of, and does not affect or enlarge the scope, duration, ownership, or subsistence of any copyright protection in the preexisting material. The copyright in the compilation known as *Brave Women, Strong Faith*, extends only to the material contributed by the author of such work, as distinguished from the preexisting material employed in the work. Each author contributing to the work, retains the original copyright to their individual submission(s).

ISBN 978-1-949856-33-0

Watercolor illustration on cover: iStock.com/katyau

Cover design and interior typesetting by Jonathan Lewis

Printed in the United States of America

Published by Brookstone Publishing Group
P.O. Box 211
Evington, VA 24550

DEDICATION

This debut edition of *Brave Women Strong Faith* is dedicated in in memory of SSG Michael H. Simpson and Galen Norsworthy, a former Army Ranger, retired pastor, and businessman.

Sergeant Michael Simpson gave his life in service to his country, leaving a legacy of love through his beloved wife, Krista Simpson, and their two beautiful sons, Michael and Gabriel.

We acknowledge his sacrifice and the strength of those who miss him most.

"Greater love has no one than this, that someone lay down his life for his friends."
John 15: 13 ESV

Galen Norsworthy was the beloved husband of Lita Norsworthy, and a father. He was also a father to many sons and daughters in the faith. His belief in Jesus moved us and his compassion for others inspired us to action. His commitment to share the freedom held within the gospel spurred us forward to see The Great Commission fulfilled in our day. He is sorely missed, but we rejoice that he is home with his Father in Heaven.

"Now I would remind you, brothers, of the gospel I preached to you, which you received, in which you stand, and by which you are being saved, if you hold fast to the word I preached to you—unless you believed in vain. For I delivered to you as of first importance what I also received: that Christ died for our sins in accordance with

the Scriptures, that he was buried, that he was raised on the third day in accordance with the Scriptures..."

1 Corinthians 15: 1-5 ESV

ACKNOWLEDGEMENTS

THIS BOOK IS about introducing the military narrative into the mainstream culture. Our stories are unique and powerful. In these untold tales, we carry daily burdens boldly and hoist ourselves into marching forward against adversity—in peace time and at war.

I am beyond grateful for the ability to share in this project with some of the most compassionate women. These warrior writers exemplify the prototype of talented and gifted communicators who have dedicated their giftings to glorify God.

To My Family: Keith, thank you for serving faithfully alongside of me, for leading our family well, and ordering more pizza than any man should. To Hannah, Beau, Noah, and Carole, thank you for being patient and giving Mommy grace for all of the office hours this project required. It is finally finished!

To My Battle Buddies: Danielle Whalen, Marla Bautista, Laura Schofield, Chandee Ulch, Aj Smit, Kennita Williams, Jessica Manfre, Kara Ludlow, Jolynn Lee, Amanda Huffman, Jessica Briggs, Megan Harless, Richelle Futch, Grace Tuesday, Brittani Emmorey, Sherry Eifler, Wendi Iacobello, Sonia Garza, and Becky Hoy. God has called all of you to life-giving task of being a herald, a proclaimer of the gospel, for our community and our country. The confirmation of this call is clear, and I hope upon the completion of this anthology, you will all step forward in confidence- knowing that you are each anointed and appointed to the task.

To Carol Kent: Saying "thank you" doesn't even begin to express the deep and abiding gratitude I have for you or for your willingness to partner with us in the advance of Christ's Kingdom here on earth. You caught the vision of a mission-minded military community. With your invaluable investment in me as a leader, and with your encouragement for a generation of military spouse ministers, leaders, and free-thinkers, you have launched a movement that I believe will change the world. Thank you for your wisdom, your servant's heart, your obedience to God in shepherding the *Speak Up Conference*, and for pointing us always back to Jesus.

To Brookstone Publishing Group: None of this would be possible without your innate desire to share the military story and support a group of rag-tag rowdy women. Thank you for being our "Publishing Parents," guiding and encouraging us to be bold.

Founders, Suzanne and Shawn Kuhn: Your belief in us spurs us forward. Thank you for jump-starting this journey.

Project Manager, Anita Brooks: We cannot tell you how deeply we appreciate your dedication to see this project through. Your insight, guidance, and flexibility has made this job a complete and total joy.

Executive Editor, Karen Jordan: The contribution that you have made toward growing and developing the authors that penned these pages is immeasurably appreciated. From the bottom of our hearts, we thank you.

To Galen and Lita Norsworthy: There are people that God graciously knits together for His glory and our good. We, as a collective military community, know that both of you have been placed in our path on purpose. As Kingdom workers, it is obvious that you have helped and healed so many. We love you.

To Our Military Community Editors: MilSpo Co. exists to help change the narrative surrounding our military spouse community. We labor underneath the hope that our stories will reach wide and inspire people to faith. MilSpo Co. is the vehicle and all of you are most certainly the road. Thank you for your unending support, enthusiasm, and sisterhood.

Kariah Manwaring, Lead Digital Marketing Specialist, Military Spouse Magazine: You're the best. Thank you for being such a positive voice and sounding board for us all.

Tessa Robinson, Managing Editor, We Are the Mighty: You are an inspiration to us all. With your uplifting disposition, and unlimited talent, our community thrives because of you.

Rebecca Alwine, Spouse & Family Editor, Military.com: We are blessed to see you sharing your gifts and talents. You have been a consistently positive communicator in our space, and we are expectantly waiting as God continues to grow you—and your platform.

Bianca Strzalkowski, Managing Editor, AmeriForce Media: You have been such a fierce advocate for us all. You have encouraged us, inspired many, and continue to push us forward.

To Our Biggest Cheerleaders: There is an African Proverb that I think about when I reflect on all of the amazing people on this journey with us. It reads "If you want to go fast, go alone. If you want to go far, go together." You keep us fearlessly inching forward, knowing that we take each step from a place of empowerment.

Lori Simmons, Vice President & Chief Marketing Officer at Armed Forces Insurance: This generation of military spouses will leave a legacy of Kingdom work and unshakable faith because of your obedience to the Lord and your love for us. Because of you, we have been unified in such a powerful way. I know that the MSOY community will move mountains for Jesus.

Curtez Riggs, Founder of the Military Influencer Conference: There is no doubt in my mind that the world as we know it has been changed because of you. Your dedication to amplify our military community voices has resulted in an explosion into the mainstream culture. You have elevated this community and call us all to join the fight. Thank you for fearlessly leading and shepherding this community.

To Our MSOY Family: Krista Anderson, Kristen Christy, Stacy Bilodeau, Shelia Brookins, Brian Alvarado, Brittany Boccher, Flossie Hall, Moni Jefferson, Maria Reed, Samantha Gomolka, Ingrid Yee, MJ Boice, Corie Weathers, and Amber Conroy: Keep shining brightly.

To My Closest Crew: Katie Byrd, Laura Early, Andi Adams, Lindsey Litton- Thank you for all of the late-night calls, last minute video vent sessions, and fast food support. I couldn't have held it together without you.

Lastly, To the *Speak Up Conference* Family: Your radical hospitality and abundance of love has changed our lives. You have stepped up to the plate of caring for and nurturing growth in each of our giftings, propelling us forward. Because of you, Speak Up is the event of the year.

To Susan Call: You are the reason I write and the first person to make me believe that I could answer God's calling on my life as a writer and biblical communicator.

To Sandi Banks: Your passion for writing is contagious and your instruction has been instrumental in developing a writing craft that overflows out of a love for Jesus.

To Robyn Dykstra: Your smile and sunny disposition constantly reflects the abounding love of Christ. In all you do, He shines through you.

To Anne and Don Denmark: When I stumbled my way into that first faculty dinner, both of you made me feel more seen, wanted, and cared for than in any other space. Thank you for your continued encouragement and support.

To Bonnie Emmorey: None of us could have accomplished any of this without your willingness to serve alongside of us. Thank you for always answering the phone, giving wise counsel, praying for us, and being an exemplary woman of faith. Your friendship has been one of the greatest gifts.

LETTER FROM THE PUBLISHER

THROUGHOUT THE BIBLE, Scripture refers to sowing seed in good soil and seeing a harvest. This project is the fruit resulting from a scholarship seed planted by Hans Kuhn and Dana Kuhn two years ago, allowing five military spouses to attend the *Speak Up Conference*. That first year, those five scholarships grew into seventeen, affirming the fertile ground they found. The following year, the Kuhn brothers and others, including Galen and Lita Norsworthy, for whom the scholarship is now named, funded over fifty scholarships. They also provided monies to help see this book published.

As parents of a Navy son who serves in the chaplain's office, we know the sacrifice our daughter-in-law and grandchildren make, while their husband and father concentrates on contributing to the greater good of our nation. This gives us a heart, as well as understanding, for what the brave women represented in this book describe in their true accounts of personal service and fortitude.

But this book displays so much more than stories of sacrifice and resilience, it spotlights women who are people of purpose. The giving visionaries behind the scholarship fund and this publishing project see the potential of these extraordinary women. They can reach beyond their military life challenges and impact their bases, neighborhoods, and hence the world, for the Kingdom of God. We are honored to publish this book and pray that as seeds are planted through the pages of this manuscript, a harvest of a hundredfold or more is realized.

Suzanne & Shawn Kuhn and the Brookstone Creative Group/Brookstone Publishing Group Teams

CONTENTS

Dedication	ix
Acknowledgements	xi
Letter From the Publisher	xvii
Foreword	xxiii
Introduction	xxvii

PART ONE
MISSIONS AND MOVING: THE MILITARY LIFE

Chapter One: The Gift I Never Wanted	
Becky Hoy	3
Chapter Two: Breaking the Confinement	
Jessica Manfre	9
Chapter Three: Military Families Just Want to Belong	
Megan Harless	15
Chapter Four: The Power of Community and Connection	
Sonia Garza	21
Chapter Five: Stuck in the Middle	
Brittani Emmorey	27

PART TWO
THE TIES THAT BIND: MARRIAGE AND MOTHERHOOD

Chapter Six: The End is Just the Beginning	
Jessica Briggs	35
Chapter Seven: Surf Lessons	
Kara Ludlow	43
Chapter Eight: My Rainbow Calls Me Mommy	
Marla Bautista	53

Chapter Nine: Sacrifice
Chandee Ulch — 59

Chapter Ten: Home is Where the Marine Corps Sends You
Jolynn Lee — 65

PART THREE

FRIENDS THAT BECOME FAMILY: RELATIONSHIPS AND COMMUNITY

Chapter Eleven: How a Red Tent Became a Place for Soul Food
Aj Smit — 75

Chapter Twelve: Stronger Together
Sherry Eifler — 81

Chapter Thirteen: Grieving Broken Things
Megan Harless — 87

Chapter Fourteen: My Village. Our Village.
Marla Bautista — 93

Chapter Fifteen: You Are Your Circle
Kennita Williams — 99

Chapter Sixteen: Step Forward in Faith
Sonia Garza — 105

PART FOUR

HEROES THROUGH HEARTBREAK: GRIEF, LOSS, AND POST TRAUMATIC STRESS

Chapter Seventeen: No Greater Gift
Chandee Ulch — 113

Chapter Eighteen: Life is What Happens
Grace Tuesday — 121

Chapter Nineteen: How to "Lean In" to the Pain of Others
Jolynn Lee — 127

Chapter Twenty: The Journey Through Loss, Infertility, and God's Miracles
Wendi Iacobello — **133**

Chapter Twenty-One: Loving, Leaving, and Learning
Becky Hoy — **141**

Chapter Twenty-Two: A Sorrow Shared is But Half a Trouble
Jolynn Lee — **147**

Chapter Twenty-Three: Digging for Treasure
Grace Tuesday — **155**

PART FIVE
TIME TO SPEAK UP: MILITARY MISSION WORK AND ADVOCACY

Chapter Twenty-Four: A Mission of Kindness
Jessica Manfre — **163**

Chapter Twenty-Five: In the Moment
Sherry Eifler — **171**

Chapter Twenty-Six: Where Two or More Are Gathered
Aj Smit — **177**

Chapter Twenty-Seven: Faith Unfolded
Chandee Ulch — **183**

PART SIX
CUT FROM THE SAME CLOTH: THE WARRIOR WOMEN

Chapter Twenty-Eight: Finding Purpose Again
Amanda Huffman — **191**

Chapter Twenty-Nine: A Dream Deferred
Laura Schofield — **197**

Chapter Thirty: From Service to Finding Your Calling
Megan Harless — **205**

Chapter Thirty-One: The Garments I Have Worn
Danielle Whalen — **211**

Chapter Thirty-Two: A Legacy of Valor
Megan Brown — **217**

Chapter Thirty-Three: Warrior Within — Leading Myself
Sherry Eifler — **223**

Chapter Thirty-Four: A Call to Step Boldly
Richelle Futch — **229**

Epilogue: The Warrior Archetype
Danielle Whalen — **237**

FOREWORD

BY CAROL KENT

IT WAS THE fall of 1999 and I was headed to Frankfurt, Germany. The Protestant Women of the Chapel had invited me to speak at *Faithlift*, a five-day conference for mil-spouses and active duty women in the military from our U.S. bases all over Europe. I was picked up at the airport and driven two hours further inland to a beautiful hotel in the ski resort town of Willingen.

Four hundred women were gathering for an inspirational getaway with their military sisters. Many drove long hours from their bases. Some came on chartered buses. Others arrived on military transport planes. As I entered the lobby, enthusiasm was high.

One young woman could be heard above the rest. "Our bus broke down in the middle of nowhere and it took several hours for the missing parts to arrive. While we waited, we sang worship songs on the bus, and then we took turns telling about how we came to faith in Jesus Christ. And by the time the needed parts arrived, we led our bus driver to the Lord." Loud cheers could be heard.

I loved these women almost instantly. They were like sisters to each other. Most of them were far from home, overseas for a minimum of two years, separated from their biological families. They clung to each other, confided in one another, and celebrated their friendships. There was an unmistakable loyalty in these women. Because of orders from Uncle Sam, they were in a foreign land—but they were not alone. They had each other.

It was my assignment to do the Bible teaching at a main group session each day, but I had also volunteered to teach a workshop from the *Speak Up Conference* called, "I Have a Story to Tell." It was a talk on how to prepare your personal testimony of how you came to know Christ as your Savior. On the third day of the conference, I walked into a tightly packed hotel conference room.

The women paid close attention as I spoke on the essential points to include when summarizing your story. Then I shared what to include in a prayer when you're leading people to invite Christ into their lives and I felt led to say, "For some of you, this might be the first time you've heard how you can begin a relationship with Jesus. If you'd like to do that now, please pray silently as I speak aloud." I led the women in confession of sin, in an acknowledgment that Jesus paid the price for their sins when He died on the cross, and in an opportunity to invite Christ into their lives. Seven young military spouses said "Yes" to Jesus that day.

The next morning, I was on the third floor of the hotel walking toward my room when I heard a voice behind me saying, "Carol, can you help us? Heather wants to become a Christian, but we can't remember all of the words of that prayer."

I followed the young woman to the room where Heather was standing in the doorway. Her hair was a mess and she was smoking as if her life depended on it. She obviously hadn't had much sleep. Heather thought she wanted to become a Christian, but now that the keynote speaker was at her door, everything was a little scary. Several milspouses were also there. I suggested that we move into one of the rooms and sit on the beds so we could talk.

The women were eager to have Heather become a "sister in Christ." I began by saying, "Why don't we start by having some of you share how you came to faith?" A hand shot into the air as a young milspouse said, "I was religious for my whole life, but it wasn't until I came to this conference that I found out you need to make it personal. I just invited Jesus into my life one hour ago." One by one all of the other women shared about the difference Christ had made in their lives.

By this time Heather had gone through half a pack of cigarettes, while listening intently. I spoke. "Heather, after everything you've heard these women share, would you like to become a Christian?" She took one last drag on her cigarette and shook her head with an affirmative nod. This affirming group of military women stood up and made a circle. They locked arms around each other, with two of them on both sides of Heather, as she began to pray aloud.

> *God, I'm a mess. You know I've been sleeping around on my husband while he's been away from the base, and I need your forgiveness in my life. I know that Jesus paid the price for my sin when He died on the cross, and I know He rose again. Please come into my life and save me. Amen.*

The women embraced Heather and celebrated. Then Susan, the woman who invited Heather to the conference, put her arms around her and sang a song of welcome into the body of Christ. They had met in the commissary and both of them had daughters named Harley. They tried to get together a few times, but Susan was so "Christian," and Heather was not. With very little in common, they hadn't seen each other in a while. But Susan invited Heather to attend *Faithlift*, and Heather thought: *Hmm . . . free babysitting on the base, five days away in a lovely hotel, no meals to prepare—even if this event is religious, I'd like to go*. And that's how two milspouses became sisters in Christ at a ski resort in Germany.

After that event, I was hooked on spending as much time as possible with women connected to the military. I went back to Germany two more times, and then I was asked to speak at

Faithlift at Yongsan Military Base in Seoul, S. Korea. I returned one more time for that event, and then made a separate trip back to S. Korea to teach communication skills to military women in ministry leadership. Following that, it was a privilege to travel to several of the conferences sponsored by the PWOC for military women all over the U.S.A.

Then, about three years ago, I met Megan Brown, a military spouse and a fireball for Jesus, who was attending the *Speak Up Conference* in Grand Rapids, Michigan. By that time, we offered a speaking track and a writing track, and I sensed her passion for getting other milspouses trained as global military missionaries—and last year we had seventeen women from the military community attend. This year we expect about one hundred women in the military community to join us for our first-ever virtual training.

Out of that conference, a book has been birthed and it's written by brave women who have strong faith. You'll find their stories captivating, inspirational, heart-wrenching, and spirit-lifting. They are vulnerable, honest, and real. They tell the truth about deployment, relationships, loss, fear, mental health, isolation, and faith-shaking experiences.

Whether you are part of the military family, or someone like me who deeply appreciates the sacrifices of these women, this book will make you more compassionate, more prayerful, and more grateful for the difference a strong faith in God brings to every challenge we face. I hope you'll buy one book for yourself and ten more to give away. This book is worthy of your time.

Carol Kent, Author and Speaker
Founder of the *Speak Up Conference*
www.carolkent.org
www.SpeakUpConference.com

INTRODUCTION

BY MEGAN B. BROWN

WHAT IS AN archetype? Merriam Webster defines the term to mean "the original pattern or model of which all things of the same type are representations or copies. Also; a perfect example." This book encompasses a combination of perfect examples, a picture of the core of what military women and wives are made of—the "warrior archetype." It is the stuff of heroes, battle-ridden and victorious.

In today's culture, so much of our identities are wrapped up in the service and sacrifice of our spouses. Indeed, for those of us married to the men and women who have stepped up to answer the call of their nation, it is certainly a source of our greatest pride. While deep and wide are our affections for them, our stories often end up being no more than footnotes in the shadows of their choice to serve.

This anthology is a collection of *our* stories, a memoir of the scars that we bear on our own bodies from our choice to stand and serve beside them. We believe in the same noble causes that inspired them to fight and we, as well, are ardent patriots. The price of liberty is worthy of the cost of our loneliness. Freedom trumps the need of living close to family and lifelong friends. We respond to these beliefs by making the choice to sacrifice.

We pack up, buck up, and bubble-wrap our own emotions in order to follow God's calling into uncertainty.

We as a whole, want our communities and our country to see who we are. We also want to share these truths with those who would come behind us—to leave a legacy of encouragement for the military spouses that are hot on our heels. We want you to know that we are bold, brave, fierce, exhausted, broken, and hurting. We aren't only married to warriors; we are the warriors.

Our goal in collecting and compiling this anthology is to share a deep and authentic insight into the inner workings of our lifestyle and to impart ways that we could build a bridge between the military and civilian communities. This bridge is imperative for what is to come.

WE PACK UP, BUCK UP, AND BUBBLE-WRAP OUR OWN EMOTIONS IN ORDER TO FOLLOW GOD'S CALLING INTO UNCERTAINTY.

I believe there is a revival on the horizon, a gospel explosion that will sweep the world. I also believe that the military community will be vital and essential in the implementation of this revival. We are perfectly positioned for this purpose. We have the capacity and capability to play an active part in the restoration and renewal of the world as we know it.

Military members and their families make magnificent missionaries. We move every two to four years (paid for by the U.S. Government), embody extreme resilience, and are innately mission-minded. If properly equipped, we could very likely carry the redemptive story of Jesus Christ to the four corners—to the ends of the earth.

In order to see The Great Commission fulfilled in our day, we need you. If you are a fellow member of the military community, we need you to join our ranks in the largest Kingdom army ever imagined by living as a sent ambassador for Christ. If you are a civilian and a member of the local church, we need you to advocate for us in your local body of believers—to see us, meet some of our unique needs, and plug us in to the life of your local congregation. Help us build community and then send us out for the mission and purpose of Jesus.

As you spend time soaking in these stories, I pray your heart would be moved into action. As these warriors begin to bare their souls, ask God what He would have you do in response. Would He have you welcome someone new or encourage someone who is struggling? Or would He equip you to share the truth of His Word, freeing people in Jesus' name? Whatever the response, I pray these stories bless you and call you into a deeper love of Christ.

Part One

MISSIONS AND MOVING: THE MILITARY LIFE

Chapter One
THE GIFT I NEVER WANTED

BECKY HOY

I'M NOT SURPRISED that so many movies are made about soldiers in battle. A classic "military life" tale is so inspiring it's impossible not to be captivated by it.

There's something thrilling about a soldier who sacrifices his own happiness to leave those he loves at home. In movies, we often see him touching down with his fellow service members in a foreign land, ready to fight for freedom, while having an action-packed epic adventure. Sometimes, the hero completes his journey with a beautiful homecoming, sometimes with trials or tragedies. But no matter the ending, it's an exhilarating story.

There's a reason that movies are generally not made about life on the home side of deployment.

For military spouses awaiting the return of their service members, the story arc is just not as enthralling, or at least it wouldn't appear so. From the outside looking in, those holding down the home front simply continue with regular life. They complete the tasks and responsibilities of each day sans one set of hands to help out. To the naked eye, the deployment season looks for military spouses much like any other season of life, just with a bit of loneliness and extra worry sprinkled in. And yet, as in so many things, the true adventure of living with a deployed spouse lies so much deeper than what you can observe on the surface.

You see, the world really loves the image of a passive military spouse—yellow ribbon in hair, she waits for her loved one to return. Even as the role of a military spouse has evolved to include business owners, career-pursuers, adventurers, and artists of every gender, this stereotype continues to resurrect the quintessential "good housewife" cliché, and the general public is nothing short of here for it. The term "military spouse" has become synonymous with the idea of waiting passively—enduring the struggle—until your missing half returns to make you whole.

At the start of my husband's first deployment, I had internalized this exact image. With my only exposure to life as a military family having come from films and stories, I walked into the first days of his deployment seeing myself as a passive participant. This season of separation was simply happening around me, and there were just a few realities I needed to come to terms with.

I took stock of the little I knew and tried hard to accept my necessary reality. I knew I would be sad. I knew I would be lonely. I knew there would be extra to manage in our household. Quite plainly, I knew this season was going to be miserable, but I was a military spouse. So, I decided it was my job to *endure*.

Yes. I would push through the loneliness. I would embrace the sadness. I would work hard to keep the household moving forward. Like the good military spouses I was acquainted with, I could do this. I. Would. Endure.

But I found out quickly that enduring simply was not going to cut it.

Within weeks of his departure, I realized that every movie, TV show, and storybook ever written had told me military spouses should learn to "endure" their spouse's deployment. Enduring this season meant living in the stereotypical reality of the military spouse who "waits on the one they love." It painted this season of separation as something to be tolerated, to be survived and wished away.

I considered how many times I could tolerate this kind of separation, and it hit me—*My husband had chosen the military as his career.* There was no turning back.

This season of deployment would be a regular part of my life for the foreseeable future, and I knew I didn't want to just "endure" the days or wish them away. This was my life now and I wanted to stop surviving, so I could start thriving.

At that moment of clarity, the most amazing thing happened. My entire paradigm around my spouse's deployment shifted. I decided I would reclaim this season of separation. I would not be a passive participant, but instead, I would make the most of this challenge. If someone did dare to create a movie about the home side of a deployment, my character would stand in my living room with an instrumental track swelling ever louder as a camera panned to highlight the determined stare on my face. My resolved stance would provide a clear picture of our heroine ready to conquer the deployment-sized mountain in front of her.

With that simple change in perspective, the truth of life as a military spouse became clear. I had not been placed here to become a docile sufferer, enduring the difficulties, and waiting for the next reunion. I had been placed here to embrace a unique opportunity to grow in ways unimaginable.

I tossed the yellow ribbon out of my hair, and I began the

work of reclaiming each day while my spouse was deployed. (Okay, I didn't actually have a yellow ribbon in my hair to toss. But if this were a movie, I would have.) Motivated by this new perspective, I chose to thrive. I knew it would change me. But I had no idea it would change my marriage.

Exchanging my sadness for friendship, I crafted a new ability to connect with those around me. Deployment forced me to step outside of my comfort zone, forge new relationships, and create my own "finding my best friend" montage in the movie of my life. When he returned home, my husband discovered a circle of new friends who had supported me, and who had been silently cheering him on every step of the way.

I HAD BEEN PLACED HERE TO EMBRACE A UNIQUE OPPORTUNITY TO GROW IN WAYS UNIMAGINABLE.

Exchanging my worry for action, I pushed myself to prioritize my own wellness, so I could become mentally and physically tough in a season so apt to break you down. I overcame my own self-doubt to achieve some of my greatest goals. In this part of my movie, I'm at the top of a staircase (think Rocky Balboa), crushing my own personal fight scene.

Exchanging my loneliness for long-distance love, I focused with intent on communicating carefully with my deployed spouse. I learned to read him from a distance and express love, even under the most difficult circumstances. I focused on positivity instead of complaint. I made sure I smiled more than frowned. I kept the energy in my voice upbeat, versus melancholy.

In real life, when he returned home, my husband found the most resilient and confident version of his spouse he had ever witnessed. Even before that, he experienced the new me before he landed back on American soil. After all I had accomplished while we were apart, my husband felt in person, the strength of our love forged in the fires of separation.

With a new mindset, deployment changed me, and ultimately, it changed my marriage in ways no other experience could have. Our separation was not to be endured, but embraced as a beautifully painful evolution.

Deployment is definitely not the action-packed classic we expect when it comes to military movies. But the story of this shift in the deployment paradigm, and the incredible ways it can evolve an individual and a marriage, is nothing short of stunning for the ones who walk it. It may not seem screen-worthy, and we may not follow a predictable script, but military spouses everywhere are truly the stars of this epic feature.

The next time you meet a military spouse who is on the home side of her spouse's deployment, don't ask her how she does it. Instead, ask how deployment has pushed her and her family to learn, overcome, and evolve. Grab your popcorn, sit back, and enjoy this not-so-classic tale of military life. And if you are in the starring role, take the stage with a straight spine, resolute attitude, and open heart. After all, this is your time to shine.

BECKY HOY is a U.S. Army Spouse of nine years and founder of *Brave Crate*—the deployment countdown box for military spouses. After struggling to thrive as a new military spouse during her husband, Randy's, first deployment, Becky used her background in Business Operations to carefully craft systems and routines that would allow her to reclaim the season of deployment by focusing on self-development and wellness. She is devoted to shifting the paradigm for military spouses by highlighting the unique opportunities for personal growth that the military lifestyle presents for families. Becky's work has helped to shape more than 2,000 months of deployment countdowns for military spouses and has been featured in multiple print and digital publications, including *Military Spouse Magazine* and *HuffPost*.

Chapter Two
BREAKING THE CONFINEMENT

JESSICA MANFRE

THE WEIGHT OF loneliness a new military spouse feels is almost suffocating. Waves of sadness cover them from head to toe. Sleeping makes it go away, but when they wake for the new day, the realization that they are alone again reigns. Then, that deep internal ache of despair comes and settles like lead in their stomach, pulling them down again.

No one can truly prepare you for the first time you are completely alone. But the key to surviving this lonely space is remembering this, "You'll be okay." As a matter of fact, you will go on to shine. This hard season will be nothing but a memory that prompted you to grow. I know—I was in that space thirteen years ago.

When I moved with my husband on military orders for the first time, I had never lived anywhere besides my hometown. I was a bright eyed 21-year-old, ready for adventure, thinking nothing but positive thoughts. I had this image of living a dream life with the white picket fence surrounding it.

I kissed my coastie goodbye, after spending two days together in our new home and city. Then my husband was gone. He was off to serve the mission of the United States Coast Guard. We didn't yet have cable or internet hooked up, and this was long before the days of social media.

That bright-eyed excitement faded shortly after he drove away.

The United States Coast Guard is the smallest branch of uniformed service. There are more New York City police officers than there are active duty Coast Guardsmen. This means the majority of us are stationed in areas without big military bases, and many of us live in very remote locations. This was the case for my husband and me. When he left to serve on that boat, I was alone.

The beginning of this season was utterly pitiful. There was a lot of ice cream eating, moping, and re-watching Blockbuster rentals. I could recite season one of Grey's Anatomy by heart after a few weeks—all while wearing old sweatpants and questionably stained clothes. I should add, just outside my door was one of the country's most beautiful beaches, but I was blind to everything beyond my own misery and loneliness.

While I was becoming a permanent fixture on my couch, my life was passing me by. It took me a while, but I finally realized I was losing opportunities. Although I desperately missed my spouse, I knew waiting for him to be home wasn't living.

This time in my life reminds me of what the Bible says about being strong. "He gives me new strength. He guides me in the right paths, as He has promised" (Psalms 23:3 Good News Bible). Although I didn't know it, God was giving me the courage I desperately needed. All these years later, I now know He completely saved me in those moments.

I almost drove myself home and gave up, because the isolation and loneliness felt like too much to bear. But I stayed, even when it was hard.

God led me exactly where I was meant to be. His guiding hand never left me. In Him I could trust.

God designed us with community in mind, and science has continually proven that those with close relationships have better health outcomes. Once I made the decision to build a life and not let isolation pull me down anymore, things fell into place. This was also my way of letting go and letting God lead my way.

I found myself in the midst of forced aloneness—something foreign to me before then. Growing up in a large and loud Italian family, I was never without someone to support me. But life as a mil-spouse taught me a lesson from God. He was showing me not only how strong I could be on my own, but also how to complete myself, instead of relying on others to fill me up. I discovered the only person we should truly rely on to fill any emptiness is Jesus.

How do you confront the pain of isolation and loneliness, outside of prayer? It isn't easy and actually, it's a lot of work. I missed my family. I missed my support system. I remember feeling those waves of depression from the loneliness cover me every day. I wore it like a weighted blanket in summer, heavy and uncomfortable.

It took me time to process my feelings of grief and sadness. I prayed *a lot*. I also called my grandmother every day just to hear her voice. She was a deeply faithful woman and always told me "God has a plan for you, and this too will pass." I knew she was devastated that I was no longer living at home, but even in the midst of her despair, she encouraged me to follow my path.

God knows all and even when we aren't sure, He is. "I alone

know the plans I have for you, plans to bring you prosperity and not disaster, plans to bring about the future you hope for" (Jeremiah 29:11 Good News Bible).

Once I was finally okay with being by myself, I was ready to meet people and build friendships. I surrounded myself with people and friendships that not only supported my own personal goals, but who were also striving for continual growth themselves.

When I challenged myself to get uncomfortable and put myself out there, I discovered the beauty of the military spouse friendship. In those friendships, I found instant connection and shared understanding of what this military life is really like. I had a sympathetic ear for my sadness when my husband was recalled back to the boat in the middle of our date night. Their husbands had to leave, too. Almost everything I went through, they experienced.

Milspouse friendships are priceless. When I look at new military spouses, my deepest prayer is that they will find these kinds of beautiful relationships.

Challenging myself to intentionally enter uncomfortable situations was the key to learning. You see, when you are continually comfortable, there is zero room for growth. This means saying "yes" to things you'd regularly say "no" to and trying the things you'd normally shy away from.

Chasing growth also requires a deep amount of faith, in both yourself and God's plan for you. It's also really important that in that process of exploration you get used to failing. Those painful experiences will teach you far more than getting it right every time ever will. Wear those badges of failure with honor, you will be so much better for it.

The things in life that are big and important shouldn't be easy. I liken them to a marriage—something that takes continual work, change, and growth to be successful.

As I look back over the past thirteen years as a military spouse, I know my grandmother was right all along. God had a plan and even when it was hard and uncomfortable, I stuck with it. That faith and courage would go on to define my life.

I want to go back to that 21-year-old girl and tell her so many things. If I could call her, I would tell her she's going to learn that she *can* do hard things. I would tell her that these challenging moments are going to build her into who she was meant to be. I want her to know that although she misses home with an ever-present deep ache inside, her heart is going to become so full because of beautiful friendships, and it will ease the pain of her loneliness.

> **GOD KNOWS ALL AND EVEN WHEN WE AREN'T SURE, HE IS.**

I want her to know she's going to make many mistakes along the way and that her failures won't define her. But instead, they will teach her the beauty of God's forgiveness and love. I want to say the same freeing truths to you.

Just as the Bible says, "The LORD's unfailing love and mercy shall continue, fresh as the morning, as sure as the sunrise" (Lamentations 3:22-23 Good News Bible). There's nothing you can't come back from.

We should let go of the things we've done wrong and instead focus on our commitment to get it right. While I can't truly go back to that young girl to ease her isolation and feelings of being lost without a way, I pray I can reach the new military spouse just starting her journey. I won't lie to you and tell you that parts of your story won't hurt.

There will be times that test your faith and make you question if you are on the right path. But my deepest hope is that you'll know God's love for you and hold steadfast through the pain and challenges you will surely face. Once you make it to the other side, an amazing life is waiting for you.

JESSICA MANFRE is obsessed with strong coffee and good books. You will most likely find her in a coffee shop or the library, curled up with one of her favorite stories. Jessica is a licensed social worker, freelance writer, and the co-founder of Inspire Up, a nonprofit dedicated to serving vulnerable populations. She loves Jesus and is a strong vocal advocate on veteran and military family issues. Jessica's husband is currently in active duty, serving in the United States Coast Guard. They currently reside in Illinois with their son, daughter, two dogs, multiple fish, and two lizards.

Chapter Three
MILITARY FAMILIES JUST WANT TO BELONG

MEGAN HARLESS

HAVE YOU EVER had a military family move into your neighborhood? Maybe you met one at church or in your child's class. Did you reach out and say "hi?" Invite them to coffee or attempt to get to know them? Did you think it was weird that you had a military family in your neighborhood? Particularly, if they do not move near a big military base, they are probably living in an uncommon area for them and on some special assignment, feeling like a fish out of water.

Service members and their families are used to the nomadic life. It's part of their norm. Every few years, we have our houses packed up by complete strangers, loaded onto trucks, and delivered in some far-off corner of the world—to a place where we will likely know no one. We will have no family nearby, no friends waiting for us, and we will do our best to try and find where we might fit in.

My husband is nearing fifteen years of active duty service, and during that time, we have seen 10 PCS's (Permanent Change of Station), four years of being dual military, five deployments between us, and our oldest of three children in the sixth grade is attending his sixth school in the fifth state we've lived in. We move on average every 18-24 months. It may sound crazy, but it's the life of service we chose.

THE TRUTH IS, MILITARY FAMILIES ARE NOT MUCH DIFFERENT FROM YOU AND YOUR FAMILY.

Many times, when we PCS, it is from one military installation to another. We have post resources available, and we just join new chapters of the organizations we were a part of at our new location. Often, life finds a way to seemingly continue from point "a" to point "b" with little to no hiccups. But then there are times when we get sent to a "remote" location. No, it is not always off in the middle of the desert or in a tundra of a foreign country, even though it feels like it. Remote means we are sent to a location that doesn't have a *normal* military base. It is either a recruiting station, a small depot with a high civilian population, or a national guard post. It means we are thrown into living a civilian life without our military peers, organizations, or resources. For some, that may not seem like a big deal, but for a spouse or family used to a constant up tempo, hustle and bustle life, this can be very scary.

The first time we lived at a remote location, we were twenty minutes south of a major city, and we were parents of a newborn baby. We had no family or friends there. Everyone in the area who was military affiliated were national guard, and they already had their friends and family to rely on. In our three years at that assignment, it took me nearly eighteen months before I met my first friend.

During those eighteen months, I had everything I needed but the solitude made me feel utterly alone. I didn't have that friend down the street who came over to hang out, or the neighbor who provided dinner when we brought one of our children home from the hospital. There was no church group that prayed me through deployment the first time. The isolation made me reserved, quiet, and sheltered in a way that also killed any identity and purpose I once had.

Currently, we are living at a remote location again. I lovingly refer to it as the wilderness—or Podunk. It was not my first choice of locations, and I may have come kicking and screaming, but I also arrived with an open mind, full of optimism for the children. We are assigned to a little depot in the corner of Texas. There are only a few active duty folks here, and it's a community that does not seem to know what to do with us. Everyone who lives here has grown up here. They have their friends, family, and traditions. They know the ins and outs of where to go and what to do.

When we first moved in, we reached out to meet our neighbors. This is our second time living in a remote location, and over the years, I've learned how important it is to connect with people and build your support group. When we arrived, I was eager to meet a friend or at least find a friendly face. My optimism was quickly smothered by the responses we heard.

"Why would you move here?"

"You have moved how many times?"

It was like a knife to my heart. No one understood. And when we mentioned where my husband worked, they were all surprised to hear there were any active duty military people at the depot down the road.

In the past six to seven months, I have made a few friends, including someone I can call for family emergencies. When moving into an area where everyone already knows everyone, it's hard breaking into a circle and connecting with people. Sometimes as a military family, we don't want to get attached, because we know it will only be a short time until we move again. Other times, it's the locals who don't want to let us in, because we'll be moving on soon. When this happens, all miss out on any potential joy and memories.

The truth is, military families are not much different from you and your family. Sure, we move a lot, there's no hiding that. But there is so much more to us. We know how to be resilient and resourceful. We'll easily repurpose those old curtains into new throw pillow covers if you want our help. We'll make a pantry out of any closet and match wall paint colors like we are Bob Ross. Somewhere in our military life experience, we learned how to fix a leak, change a tire, and install a dishwasher or water heater, and can assist with your sudden emergency.

Military families have learned how to make celebrating Christmas in July just as special as if it were happening in December. A spouse will drop everything at a moment's notice to bring you dinner on your worst day, sit with you through the pain, or watch your children while you run to the ER. They will squeeze a baseball team of children into their small home to celebrate, let you have date night, or host the comfort of gathering friends.

As a military family, we want what you want. We want to belong, to have someone we can call in an emergency, or to vent to. We want our children to make friends and form those lifelong bonds. We want to love the place we are living at and to be dragged away crying because of the impact you left on our hearts. We want to remember each station as a season of joy, happiness, and growth. We want to be part of the community, too.

We yearn for the day when we can show up at a location and find a community that takes us in and makes us as one of theirs. We want the community the Bible so vividly describes.

Romans 12:16 tells us we should, "Live in harmony with one another." Romans 15:7 also says, "Therefore welcome one another as Christ has welcomed you communities." Lastly, 1 John 4:11 says, "Dear friends, since God so loved us, we also ought to love one another."

We long for community where we don't have to worry about making it on our own, and can know that our seat at that table was saved and waiting for us. Ultimately, Scripture teaches us that love, above all other things, is what we as believers should strive for. We love you. Please help us to feel seen, loved, and wanted in return.

MEGAN HARLESS is an Army veteran, military spouse, mom to three amazing children, and is committed to educating others on the regulations and policies of PCS (permanent change of station) while working on reform efforts to streamline and simplify the process for military families. She graduated from the University of Charleston, WV where she met her husband and commissioned as a Transportation Officer, where she went on to serve 4 years as a dual active duty family to include one deployment to Iraq.

When she hung up her uniform for the last time, she gracefully slipped into the role of military spouse, where she has supported her husband. As a family they have PCS'd ten times in the past 14 years. Megan has worked with members of Congress, US Transportation Command, and members of the moving industry to identify key pain points of the process and to draft solutions to be implemented for families. During this time, she has become the leading Military Spouse PCS expert and received the 2020 Military.com Spouse Changemaker of the Year award.

Chapter Four
THE POWER OF COMMUNITY AND CONNECTION

SONIA GARZA

I'D LIKE TO tell you a story—a story about a house. This is not just any house, but truly a house so special it compelled me to tell you about the many blessings it has bestowed upon us these past five years. It is the house across the street.

In 2015, we had just moved to our home in Dupont, Washington, a little town right outside the gates of Joint Base Lewis-McChord, a combined Army/Air Force installation in Washington state. Now, I say "we" like both my husband and I moved our home, but that was not the case. It rarely ever is in military life. As luck would have it, when we purchased our second house, he was on a deployment. I was signing closing documents from the states, while he was taking trains to the Embassy to get his documents notarized.

We had a son, Diego, who was one-and-a-half years old. I was three months pregnant with our daughter, and it was time to move from our townhouse thirty minutes away, to our new home.

How was I supposed to move by myself? Relocating across town, lifting heavy boxes, and unpacking a million items while in the first trimester of pregnancy. *What could be stressful about that?* I decided it might not be too bad. After all, other spouses had packed up their homes and PCS'd (or Permanent Change of Station), while their husbands were gone.

With God's amazing grace and to my absolute surprise, both soldiers and military spouses mobilized to help me when I needed it most. Spouses showed up, rolled up their sleeves, and packed up my belongings. Soldiers from my husband's battalion carried our heaviest items and shared the loads. It was truly a miracle, and I will always remember the power of the military community in that moment.

Once we moved in, I felt peace. I knew we were "home," or whatever that meant, for as long as we'd be there. I prayed constantly, asking God to bless our new home and the homes around us. As a military family, having good neighbors, people to rely on and do life with, will make or break the experience of a local duty station. I knew we needed friendship and community, but I did not expect the immense blessings that God sent us through the house across the street.

From the first time I met the renters of that house, I knew the wife and I would be close friends, and it happened quickly. We were in the same stage of life together—stay-at-home moms to multiple babies and living day-to-day. We shared and savored the daily routines together, and that was my saving grace. Whether it was someone to come watch my kids in an emergency or simply a need for a stick of butter, she was there.

Dirty hands from the neighborhood kids smudged the surface of my storm door, and looking back, those tiny smudges are imprinted on my heart forever. When our neighbors across the street were relocated because of military orders, my son ran after their van. It broke my heart to know our friendship had evolved so much, and now they were leaving. As their van pulled away, we sat and cried. We allowed ourselves to feel sad, and then said another silent prayer that whomever occupied the house across the way would be another blessing to our family.

That summer, God was faithful, as He always is, and a new family moved in. While my husband was on yet another deployment, my children and I marched over, with freshly baked cookies in hand. They've now lived in that house for three years and have become our closest friends—in good times and bad.

Some things have changed. The tiny hand smudges have transformed over the five years we have lived in this house. They moved up the door, as short kids have grown. Those little hands mean children came in and out, while enjoying our home. They represent playmates for my children to do this crazy military life with. The one thing that hasn't changed is the love shared between two neighboring homes.

As we near another summer of deployments and endure another PCS season (summertime is usually when the military moves our forces around) our neighbors will move, and others will soon occupy "the house." I know how crucial community is in this season. I continue to ask God to bless that house across the street, knowing a new family will be coming in a few short months.

Having neighbors that are friends—but more than that—having neighbors who know the absolute power of connection, is imperative to thriving in this life. This has kept my family afloat. Our neighbors are our family.

It takes finding your "tribe," your sisterhood of women spouses, who have been down that same path as you and are willing to walk alongside life's journey with you, to survive. Had I kept my door closed and my heart shut to the possibility of connection, I would have missed out on that pivotal life lesson we military spouses are lucky enough to learn.

Military life forces us to make the most of our time in any given situation, because we know time is precious. We know we may only have one year, or three at most, to form the bonds of sisterhood that will carry us through the stages of living we share—and beyond. This experience is reserved for the military community. We are fortunate enough to have this gift, despite the heartache that follows in its wake.

> **HAVING NEIGHBORS THAT ARE FRIENDS— BUT MORE THAN THAT— HAVING NEIGHBORS WHO KNOW THE ABSOLUTE POWER OF CONNECTION, IS IMPERATIVE TO THRIVING IN THIS LIFE.**

The civilian population may never have the chance to make the most of their neighbors. Equipping ourselves with this knowledge allows us to dive in and love deeply. We are the way-finders, being moved from base to base, community to community, growing in our love and faith for the mission at hand. We are the ones who dig our feet in and plant temporary roots, sometimes begrudgingly and with tears, but mostly with smiles.

You see, we know the power of community and connection. We are the women that bring cookies to a neighbor moving in. We are the women that offer a shoulder to cry on when deployments get the best of us, or when Murphy's Law hits us, yet again. We are the keepers of the light, holding steadfast to our faith in the darkest times.

God gave military spouses special hearts, allowing us to shoulder the tough times and surrender to Him, but also to empower those around us. Many of us serve in more ways than we could know. We are the mighty.

We have so enjoyed these past few years in our community and are quick to count our blessings. I can remember when our street was so vacant, I thought a tumbleweed would pass by, and we live in Washington. But I have learned to trust that God is in control and will ultimately answer my prayers when loneliness darkens my spirit. I must also take charge to create the thriving community I long for.

These are the lessons I've learned and now challenge others to remember:

- Don't be afraid to show up and reach out in your communities.
- Be "the house" that everyone longs to visit.
- Be the neighbor you wish you had.
- Showing up is to be present in your time with each other. Be there—fully.
- Let your guard down and be transparent. Share your fears and difficulties.
- Reach out to those around you, even the shy and guarded.
- Hold steadfast to a mission of connection.

All of us should be bold in our pursuit of community in our neighborhoods. You never know where a new budding friendship might take you.

SONIA GARZA is a proud Army Green Beret wife of almost 12 years, mother to two, and founder and editor of *Spouse Connexion*—an online magazine platform for military spouses. A journalist by trade with a Bachelor of Arts in Communications/Journalism-Public Relations, and a Master's of Science in Nonprofit Management, her passion for writing has led her to write for print and online publications spanning from the West Coast to the East Coast. Her writing has been included in community and military post newspapers, and lifestyle magazines and military spouse blogs like *Military Spouse Magazine*, *InDependent*, *Daily Mom Military Blog*, *Army Wife 101*, MilHousing Network and more. She has lived in Texas and North Carolina and is currently stationed at JBLM, Washington. You can find her most days spending time with her family and friends and doing her favorite thing, hosting neighborhood gatherings. You can learn more about Sonia and Spouse Connexion at www.spouseconnexion.com and like Spouse Connexion on Facebook at www.facebook/spouseconnexion.

Chapter Five
STUCK IN THE MIDDLE

BRITTANI EMMOREY

THERE'S THE MILITARY world, and there's the civilian world. And somewhere in between, you'll find our family.

In 2010, two and a half years into our marriage, my husband joined the National Guard as an officer in the JAG Corps. Still in the newlywed phase, short on life experiences, and oblivious to the demands this "part-time" career would require, it rocked my world. The military lifestyle is not what I'd signed up for—and I didn't understand why my other half did.

The role of a military spouse was a far cry from where I came—and where I believed my life should head. Raised in the house my father grew up in, I first left home when I began college, located a short hour's drive from my quaint hometown. Even after embracing university life, testing my freedom, and developing a stronger sense of self, I remained a naïve, wide-eyed, timid girl. As an adult, my dreams revolved around the home. I never imagined they'd include the military.

Leaving the nest for good at the age of twenty-five and cleaving to my husband—an adventurous, driven, "What-can-I-take-on-next?" husband—forced me to rethink the perspective and patterns of my past. Together, we took on two new commitments: a commitment to each other and a commitment to serve our country. And only time would illuminate the demands of each.

While I assumed my husband's new role would act as an exciting side gig, I soon got hit with an unexpected reality: the "one weekend per month, two weeks per year" time obligation for reservists is a myth. Once my husband became a JAG officer, he was in training, mobilized, or deployed for 24 out of 36 months. And when he wasn't serving in a full-time capacity, he was required to drill, or report for duty, one weekend every month. There were also week-long training exercises, education courses, and other mandatory commitments that regularly left me home alone. But instead of embracing my independence, I resented it. With a lack of military connections, I became the odd-girl-out among civilian friends who didn't understand my loneliness. Unlike other couples, my marriage often felt like a solo sport.

With military obligations nonnegotiable, my husband and I soon became accustomed to celebrating birthdays, wedding anniversaries, and other important milestones over the phone instead of over candlelight dinners. As I began to realize how much time the Guard truly required, I struggled to reconcile my expectations with reality. It took reassurance from my husband—and myself—to believe our relationship was his true priority, even when the military sometimes demanded first place.

By supporting my husband's dream of serving in the military, I gave up the timing of my hopes and dreams—or reluctantly allowed God to orchestrate the timeline for me. As his stint in the military progressed, I became angry that the resulting lifestyle change did not accommodate the introduction of new life into our family. Without the challenges of distance marriage or deployments, young married couples all around me were welcoming children. I hit the age of 30 childless—and with plenty of "baby envy."

Eventually, I accepted that I couldn't fully control my life's trajectory. Even so, I had yet to tackle the most daunting aspect of military life: the dreaded deployment.

Civilians and active duty soldiers alike often assume deployments are not an active concern for Reserve families. When my husband began exploring a career in the military, I distinctly remember the recruiter's fear that the unlikelihood of deployment might deter him from joining. In our newlywed state, this information was reassuring to both of us. But as my husband learned more about the inner workings of the military, he realized a deployment could accelerate his ascension up the ranks. And intending to retire with the organization, which requires twenty years of service, he was soon prepared to step up, if necessary.

> **BY SUPPORTING MY HUSBAND'S DREAM OF SERVING IN THE MILITARY, I GAVE UP THE TIMING OF MY HOPES AND DREAMS— OR RELUCTANTLY ALLOWED GOD TO ORCHESTRATE THE TIMELINE FOR ME.**

In 2012, we experienced our first deployment, and it certainly didn't count as "short" in my book. I still remember the pit in my stomach as I buried my tear-stained face against the window on the flight home from one last weekend with my husband on U.S. soil. In many terms, those next thirteen months were brutal, but I grew in ways I never thought possible. At the time, we were living near many of the unit's other spouses, and our shared experience united us.

When my husband's second deployment rolled around in the winter of 2018, however, he was attached to a different unit, and I was far from those who could best understand my circumstances. I was juggling a toddler, full-time job, and complex emotions on my own, requiring frequent visits from out-of-state family.

While we were prepared for deployments to affect us personally, we didn't foresee the toll they would take on my husband's civilian career. To date, the return from each active duty assignment has resulted in a career move for my husband, accompanied by relocation out of state. We've uprooted three times in our twelve years of marriage, almost as often as active duty members are reassigned to a new base. And while it is undoubtedly difficult to find comfort in a foreign city, it's even harder to find comfort in a new job that could easily be derailed by active duty orders.

Today, we're thousands of miles from my husband's unit and the thought of a deployment still terrifies me. But when I reflect on what we've overcome already, I see God's hand in all of it. In spite of my resentment, His redeeming love shined through. What I currently cherish most in life—meaningful relationships, my precious babies, a strengthened commitment to my military husband—has been made even sweeter because it required loss to achieve. I might always feel stuck in the middle of two different lifestyles, but with God I am committing to stand boldly between.

BRITTANI EMMOREY is a proud Mom, military spouse, and marketing professional. Brittani utilizes her writing and design talents as a Manager of Marketing Operations for a healthcare technology company. In her spare hours, she freelances as a graphic designer and communications consultant, helping non-profits advance their missions. Brittani holds a Bachelor of Arts in Communication Studies from the University of Michigan and enjoys rooting for her alma mater even during the harshest of football seasons. Brittani, her husband, and her three "dreams" (children) currently reside in Kansas.

Part Two

THE TIES THAT BIND: MARRIAGE AND MOTHERHOOD

Chapter Six
THE END IS JUST THE BEGINNING

JESSICA BRIGGS

HE WAS EIGHTEEN, fresh out of boot camp, and cleaned up from his wild high school days. We hugged hello after not seeing each other for a few years. Arthur was my best guy friend in high school, and the moment we embraced, I knew the journey would take us into unchartered waters.

Romance moved quickly between Art and me. Many critics said it was too fast, too soon. But we were already close after years of lengthy phone conversations, filling gone-by evenings with stories of hurt, hopes, and lots of 90s music. Even though we drifted apart for a while, I truly had a heart of care toward Art, remembering the brokenness he once confessed over the safety of the phone. It felt good being nice to the bad guy. But it was even more exhilarating to be in love with him.

Nine weeks after that hug, I had an engagement ring on

my finger. And six months later, we married in the little country church I grew up attending.

Three months into newlywed life, our first encounter with tragedy struck. Art's grandma, a trusted source of love and support, died suddenly after complications from an automobile accident. When the trauma unfolded, dark memories emerged from Art's past. Something changed inside my carefree husband. He shared many more details of his hurts while wading through grief, but it was just the tip of the trauma iceberg.

Emotionally, Art couldn't handle the stress his loss brought, and he quickly spun out of control, indulging in any form of self-soothing. My marriage turned dark quickly. Just months after saying "Til death do us part," a death of sorts descended on our marriage. After work, he'd sit in the guest room mentally checked out. He medicated the pain with pornography, drinking in excess, or filled his time with other indulgences. Slowly, the chasm grew between us.

We soon put all the pain and dysfunction on hold, because deployment orders came. We were a nation at war now, so we did what all military families do—we swept the junk under the rug and put one foot in front of the other. On a cold March morning, I hugged my eighteen-year-old soldier husband and drove away from base in a fog, knowing he was broken, yet heading to war.

Afghanistan's infrastructure was sparse in 2003, so our communication was limited. The two phone calls we shared over a six-month separation were full of beeping noises, static, and delay. We were lucky to get in two sentences before a mortar exploded in the background, disconnecting the call. So, I did what every good Army wife did—I wrote him a letter every day. Once a week, I demonstrated my devotion in the form of snacks and toiletries, stuffed into a care package. It seemed we were living a hero's tale, but distance and time separated the reality of our tumultuous relationship.

Six months later, we reunited. The wounds of war amplified Art's already marred past with more trauma. He was nervous to drive, on-edge, suspicious, twitching as he fell asleep, and plagued by nightmares. And his temper? It was something I'd not really seen before. He spiraled deeper into disengagement, through the screen or at the end of a bottle. Sometimes, his fists found relief through our walls and doors.

Seven months later, we repeated the same cycle. Fall apart. Deployment Orders. Pretend it's all okay. Kiss goodbye. A yearlong separation paused the pain, replacing it with the fears and experiences of Iraq. After that homecoming, the cycle repeated again, first by relocating states away. The upheaval and change triggered a cycle of anguish that seemed inescapable.

> **WE WERE A NATION AT WAR NOW, SO WE DID WHAT ALL MILITARY FAMILIES DO—WE SWEPT THE JUNK UNDER THE RUG AND PUT ONE FOOT IN FRONT OF THE OTHER.**

The third war separation really broke us. Shattered and heartbroken, barely hanging on by a thread, we said our goodbyes. We cried like never before that day—a grief and a weight neither of us could bear.

This time, we had better connections through the phone and internet. Art eventually asked me for a divorce in an instant message.

At first, I didn't take him seriously. I brushed it off as him having a bad day. I learned how serious he was when I received a phone call from a banker, asking about his joint account with another woman. Arthur was having an emotional affair.

I was shattered. By all traditional standards, I was an excellent wife. Like many broken people, I didn't know what to turn to but the faith of my childhood. One night while hot faced and covered in tears, I sensed the welcoming presence of God around me. It was like being wrapped into a big, comforting hug. He sent a message to me in that moment—that no matter what, I was loved. God's adoration so overwhelmed me, it provided a cornerstone of strength, allowing me to dismantle my perfectionism. I didn't have to be a perfect wife, I just had to be loved.

Armed with belonging through Jesus, my heart was set ablaze to demonstrate this same sort of love to Art. I let go of what I knew worked in my marriage—performance, striving, and doing my best—and I surrendered all outcomes. I didn't set out to love Art through this season to get something in return. I simply knew how loved I was, and I wanted to let that same love overflow.

While I didn't know how the story would unfold, I devised a love script of sorts, keeping my intentions clear, while communicating with Art. Instead of reacting to his cold and cutting words, the script enabled my response to remain levelheaded and gentle. Additionally, I put forth a plan to withstand his disdain for me, through affirming my identity as Beloved in Christ.

Index cards scribbled with verses accompanied me everywhere. I prayed and fasted. I sometimes ignored the emails and phone calls when I needed space. When ready to talk, I stuck to that love script—just four simple sentences: "I love you. I don't want a divorce. I won't help you get a divorce. And lastly, I love you!"

After weeks of trying to tear me down and insulting my resolve, Art realized all he had wanted was unconditional love, and he saw that was exactly what I was giving him. He confessed he wanted to stay married, but he didn't want to give up his "sins."

The counsel of the Holy Spirit whispered wise words into my soul. I repeated them to my husband. "Arthur, I'll never approve of your relationship with another woman or many of your other behaviors, but I will love you." That was enough to begin our work toward reconciliation.

I didn't know how we could repair our broken relationship. I knew boundaries needed drawn for the restoration. But I couldn't ask Art to change—he would see it as controlling. Through it all, I kept affirming my true worth and identity in Jesus, knowing I could only work on me as we moved forward.

Several weeks after reconciling, Art called me, sobbing. I could barely make out his words, and fear washed over me in waves. I was certain he wanted to call it quits again, drowning my hopes. Instead, his words blew me out of the water. He explained that he surrendered his will to Christ, and felt the weight of his burdens leave him, replaced with the gentle, easy yoke of Jesus.

Despite my own heartache and through my pain, the love of God took me on a journey to demonstrate unconditional love to Art. While Art wasn't deserving by any means, infinite love led Art to a pathway of healing in his soul. Within weeks, Art embodied the putting off the old self and putting on the new. He talked differently, gave up his sins, began dealing with reality head-on, and dared to dream. He felt an urgency to share this love with others, and he wanted to do that as a military chaplain.

While Art changed overnight, our marriage did not. It took many years to heal and strengthen our relationship—and for me to work through unforgiveness and for trust to be restored.

Eventually, I began sharing our testimony, hoping to inspire others to save their marriages. When suffering spouses came to me for guidance, I gave them a five-point plan, just like mine: pray, fast, memorize these verses, read these passages, and don't give up.

My plan worked for some, until a friend received heart-shattering news about her husband's repeated unfaithfulness. After sharing my "perfect plan" for redeeming marriage, it flat-out failed this time. The verses weren't comforting enough for her rent soul. The desperate prayers she whispered were left unanswered. The gusto to stay faithful was not cutting it. They got divorced.

I believe we overcome the trials of life through "the blood of the Lamb and the word of our testimony" (Revelation 12:11). Except, I translated that to mean people could heal their marriage if they followed MY words and testimony. I am ashamed I relegated the grace of God in my own marriage to a five-point plan. My pride left shattered, lonely hearts utterly exhausted from trying. Instead of showing people the same comfort and assurance of being fully loved regardless of outcomes, I gave out platitudes. Finally, I waved my white flag, surrendered my pride, stopped doling out advice, and started pointing people to the loving arms of Jesus.

After years of rebuilding, showing up, being vulnerable, pressing into our faith, and going to therapy, Art and I have learned to dance in grace and mercy, choosing love over record keeping. Having traversed the long road to resurrection in our marriage, our lives are dedicated to serving the military community with the same agape love we've found in Jesus.

Art's dream came to fruition, and he serves as a Navy Chaplain. In our community, marriages are suffering because people are suffering. The trauma many service members carry into their marriages predate war wounds. Training warriors is no insulation or guarantee for emotional success. Repeatedly sending them away from their spouse does not build resilient relationships. While the odds are stacked against our comrades, we are committed to serve them.

Our communities don't need any more five-step plans. We don't need more sermons on Ephesians 5 or doctrines that trap people in unfaithful marriages, while secretly hiding their black eyes, as the church says to "just keep trying." We don't need any more marriage small groups that teach us to perform our way into a better marriage. There's grim news in the military community, from suicide to divorce rates, and the remedies won't be found in training programs or Bible studies.

Statistics can change when people are met with unconditional love. Art and I are passionate about finding the brokenhearted within the ranks. We are privileged to love our warriors and their families the way Christ loved us—fully, completely, and without judgment.

Our ministry doesn't include five-step plans or books claiming to have the answers to save marriages. Instead, we walk in the shadow of a loving God, giving the gift of our presence. God leads in many ways—beside still waters and also along valleys of death. His Presence never leaves or forsakes. And that's the same gift we can give to others in their broken-heartedness. Whether people stay married or divorce, His love leads every step of the way. That is always the gift of love. With God, when we come to our end, we arrive at His beginning.

JESSICA BRIGGS passionately builds and shepherds authentic, biblical community. Married since 2002 to her soldier turned Navy Chaplain, the military lifestyle shaped their story of redemption and love. Now she lives to serve her community in practical ways, bridging faith with a heart for mental health. Jessica has a Masters in Counseling, which helps her uniquely minister to Army, Navy, and Marine Corps communities. She serves by preaching, teaching, counseling, equipping, and affirming. You can find her at a keyboard with a cup of coffee as she shares her thoughts and faith at www.JessicaBriggs.ink or on Instagram @eyestoseeblog.

Chapter Seven
SURF LESSONS

KARA LUDLOW

I REMEMBER TAKING IT all in. Trying to figure out military culture, since my United States Navy submariner boyfriend had just proposed. After meeting on the beach during my college spring break eight months before, I had gotten used to flying back and forth between Seattle and Honolulu. I was trying like mad to learn everything I could about the life I was headed for.

I'll never forget riding shotgun in Clint's black BMW 318i. We were driving to the Pearl Harbor Navy Exchange, a tax-free department store for military families, located in a strip mall of sorts, sandwiched between Popeye's and Subway. My eyes landed on one of the neighboring storefronts with a curious banner out front. It read, *Military Discounts on Divorce.*

I gazed at my new long-distance love in the driver's seat and couldn't fathom why someone would choose to end their marriage with a service member. I was naïve to the unique challenges and stresses military couples endure. I am sure that lawyer is not only still in business today, but he's likely added a drive-thru window.

Stress of deployments, chaotic schedules, and lives uprooted every few years will challenge even the most committed couples. But after nearly two decades, I know a thriving marriage is possible, despite constant uncertainty, courtesy of the U.S. military. We typically cannot attend weekend marriage seminars because our service members are on duty. Weekly date nights are often out because of wonky schedules. But with a staunch commitment to remaining on the same team, loads of patience and grace, and humor for days, a military marriage can serve as a refinery instead of a battleground.

And it's anything but boring.

From the minute I met Clint, until about two years into our marriage, geography was our biggest obstacle. While my friends bickered with their boyfriends and fiancés about which movie to see on a Friday night or whose turn it was to pick a restaurant for their date, I plotted arriving in the same zip code as Clint for more than a few days at a time. He was stationed on a fast-attack submarine, whose schedule was top secret. Even Clint did not receive more than a day or two's notice, before heading out to sea. He was a moving target and although I tried to anticipate when the sub would be in port, it was hard to guess correctly.

I didn't realize it then, but looking back, we learned not to be nitpicky from the beginning. Our time together always came with an expiration date, so we learned to let the little things go. We never took evening strolls around the neighborhood after cooking dinner together for granted. In the early days, you could usually find us flopped on the couch, laughing hysterically at the same old Adam Sandler movies. Guarding our time together and intentionally focusing on being present with each other, proved vital in our marriage in the years to come.

I've heard other military spouses talk about how much thought and consideration they gave to their relationship with their service member before agreeing to get married. Some weren't sure they were up for living the military lifestyle, which often means moving every few years and starting over. I'll tell you how much thought I gave to becoming a Navy wife—not one. Zero.

Here's what I knew: I was in love. I never contemplated what a Navy wife should be, could be, or was supposed to be. I knew nothing of military tradition. Clueless to unspoken rules, expectations, or responsibilities, I experienced an enormous learning curve. I was a Seattle college girl whose life was pleasantly interrupted when I happened to fall in love on spring break. We got engaged on Thanksgiving of my senior year during one of my many trips across the Pacific Ocean. Checking out the calendar that night, we agreed on an October 2001 wedding, giving us plenty of time to really get to know each other. We had spent all of six weeks together before he slipped that ring on my finger.

Wouldn't you know it, Clint received some news in March 2001 that caused us to scramble and change all of our wedding plans. His submarine was headed out on a WESTPAC (a deployment to the western pacific) that summer, and he would be gone for five to six months.

October 20th wedding? No chance.

Clint broke the news to me over the phone while I was babysitting my cousins one weekend in late March. I was devastated. We had a decision to make. We talked about whether to get married before he went underway or right after, maybe the next January. I couldn't believe it. Everything was already booked—didn't the Navy know that? And then they sent Clint off into the Pacific, leaving me alone.

Where would I live?

Would I work?

There were so many unanswered questions and scenarios. Planning the wedding for after his return seemed the logical choice. Then we could start our life together with the deployment behind us. Still mulling it over on the phone late into the night, Clint finally uttered the words that spoke straight to my heart and brought tears to my eyes. He ended our discussion on the spot, "I want my wife to meet me at the pier when I return home from deployment, not my fiancé."

In an attempt to get ahead of all of the planning, I took a moment to call my mother.

"Mom, did you talk to the Tacoma Yacht Club about changing the date of the reception to June?"

"Yes, all weekends are booked, honey. The only available dates are Thursday, June 14 or Thursday, June 21. Flag Day or Summer Solstice are your choices," Mom said.

"Hmm, let's go with the first day of summer." I gave my decision two seconds of thought.

My college graduation was set for June 12, so we had about nine days of breathing room between the two events. At least we could squeeze in a couple of pre-marital counseling sessions with our pastor. Turns out, planning a June wedding in March is possible, if you're open to a weekday.

Our last-minute, Thursday wedding, foreshadowed years and years of constant pivoting and changing plans on our calendar. Military life, I learned, meant making the most of our time together and understanding that service to the country requires relational sacrifice.

On the morning of September 11, 2001, my phone rang. Jen

said, "Have you seen the news this morning?" I was still in bed in Gig Harbor, Washington at my parents' house, half-asleep. I had answered without opening my eyes.

"No, I'm not up yet," I replied groggily.

"Never mind. Just go back to sleep," my friend said.

Now I was curious. *What was she talking about? What was so important on the news?* I stumbled into my parents' bedroom and grabbed the television remote. On every channel, I saw the horror we all saw that Tuesday morning. I watched the second plane hit, as newscasters reporting live on the air, ran for cover from smoke and flying debris. Not long after, I watched live coverage of another plane crash in a field in Pennsylvania.

I couldn't take my eyes off the news. I sat in absolute disbelief, trying to absorb the evil attacks on America. With all of the lives lost that day, news anchors on every station told viewers to "hold their loved ones a little tighter" that night. A nice sentiment, but that phrase felt like a huge punch in the gut to me.

I'd been married less than three months, and I hadn't seen my husband in six weeks. I just sat there frozen on my parents' bed for much of the day, unsure what the future would hold and feeling so very alone. That night, I curled up on the twin bed of my childhood, while my mom sat on the edge, rubbing my back. The world around me swirled with uncertainty, so I closed my eyes and snuggled in tight with my blankets, feeling like a fragile little girl.

Submarines are the silent, sneaky force in the Navy. Because operational security is absolutely necessary, the news does not report on the location of subs, nor is this information something wives are privy to. It is understood that location and dates at sea are not spoken over the phone or written in emails. The risk is simply too great.

However, the last time I'd spoken to Clint on the phone was early September. I reflected on that call.

I was at the bookstore in Gig Harbor, purchasing some reading material to help me pass the hours. Right in the middle of the transaction with the cashier, my phone rang. I kept it handy at all times for just this reason—there was no way I would miss hearing from Clint. I excused myself, waving to the cashier and blurted something about talking to my husband who's deployed. At that time, I'd hardly had the chance to use the term "husband" yet, and I proudly used the term to let people know I was a married woman.

Stepping outside onto the sidewalk of the strip mall, I hung on every word Clint said, memorizing the sound of his voice. It sounded familiar, yet I'd forgotten his unique phrases and tone. This phone call was like a shot of energy to me. Too often, I'd wondered if I'd ever hear from him again. His voice jolted my whole body and reminded me that indeed I had a husband who loved me, even if he was nowhere in the vicinity.

"The boat just pulled into Singapore," he said. "I'm enjoying the local cuisine with my buddies." It was still peace time. There was no inkling about war. Clint had traipsed around Singapore, buying a cheap suit and other souvenirs.

We talked about how much we missed each other and couldn't wait to be together again. Without being able to discuss dates or future port calls, our conversation was reduced to trading "I love yous." So, while I was dying to know the specifics of his WESTPAC, I had to be satisfied with the sound of his voice, assuring me that we would begin our life together "soon."

The morning of September 11, I was glued to the television. I didn't want to be. I wanted to go about living my life, but the pull was too strong. I was in total limbo.

When will I see Clint again?

Am I ever going to see Clint again?

How do I get my mind off the location of his submarine?

How in the world am I going to pass the hours?

Living with my parents, I felt safe but a little bored. My parents worked, my sisters had jobs, and I just hung around, waiting for the next "breaking news" headline. I needed a hobby or a job or both. Any distraction would have helped, but all I could do was wait. Wait for permission for my next move. A Navy wife for all of three months, and I was already tired of living that way.

In the October 13, 2002 edition of the Honolulu Star-Bulletin, USS Key West, my husband's assigned ship, Commander Charles Merkel recounts the notice of terrorist attacks that came via radio just after supper on September 11, 2001. *We were told to leave communication depth and make best speed to the North Arabian Sea . . . the submarine is a small place. There aren't many secrets aboard a sub, and the crew knew something had happened. I told them two planes had flown into the World Trade Center and there had been an explosion at the Pentagon.*

Without any emotional, gut-wrenching television images from the fateful day, the Key West crew immediately followed orders. They positioned themselves as the first boat within Tomahawk-missile-striking distance to targets in Afghanistan.

Even now, talking to Clint about 9/11, our perspectives couldn't be more different. My information came through the television and limited dial-up internet, thick with visual footage. My memory of 9/11 is heavy on television images, while Clint has little attachment to the footage of the twin towers collapsing. His experience of 9/11 was received though radio, which was limited to mission-critical information. He followed orders and as Commander Merkel stated, *"It was just like all the exercises we had trained for. It was successful . . . we met all our taskings."*

After that phone call outside the bookstore, it would be over two months before I'd hear Clint's voice again. And over three months until I saw him, pale and scrawny, disembarking the sub, making a beeline for me on the pier. Those reunions stick with you. In the mundane moments of life, when we are all over each other's nerves, my mind flashes back to our teary goodbyes and joy-filled reunions.

The memories matter. They remind us what we fight so fiercely to protect—our precious time together.

In her book, *Sacred Spaces: My Journey to the Heart of Military Marriage*, Corie Weathers writes, "The challenge for military families is that we sometimes walk through the greatest challenges of our lives while we are physically apart."

Clint could not fully understand how lonely I felt at my parents' house without a husband, and I will never know what it was like to be stuck underwater for months at a time without sunlight. Weathers says, "The strongest couples are those who recognize they are fighting on the same side and agree to walk through the fire together."

> **THE MEMORIES MATTER. THEY REMIND US WHAT WE FIGHT SO FIERCELY TO PROTECT. OUR PRECIOUS TIME TOGETHER.**

Clint and I have faced deployments, extended trainings, unpredictable schedules, and moves with our three kids in our marriage. Instead of becoming bitter towards each other and blaming one another for what is going wrong at any given instant, we are committed to being on the same team. And it's made all the difference. Clint and I couldn't be more opposite. I have been known to wallow in fear, playing out worst-case scenarios in my mind, while he is laid back, believing it will all work out. And yet, somehow, we balance each other out. He is my calm, and I make his back-up plans (so everything actually *will* work out). It is futile to argue about who has a harder job or whose experience was worse. It is just different. We acknowledge each other's situations, understanding that we are both doing our best with current circumstances. We depend on each other for our family to thrive and believe we are both vital to its success.

So, if we have to be creative with our time and can't commit to holiday parties or vacations, it's not because we don't want to. I still crave consistency and find myself envious of my neighbors with predictable schedules and weekly date nights. I would love to know where my kids will attend high school and put down some roots. With sacrifice comes great adventure, though. Time has proven that life cannot always be scheduled, and inevitably the waves of change are coming. Instead of fighting against the current of our circumstances, we have learned to surf—fiercely together, always.

KARA LUDLOW has been living the military lifestyle since becoming a Navy wife in 2001. She is a Pacific Northwest native currently living the California dream with her husband and three kids in sunny San Diego. She is a freelance writer whose work can be found in a variety of publications, including *Legacy* magazine, *Military Families Magazine* and *Military Spouse*.

As the former Navy Branch Coach for Jennie Allen's IF: Military, Kara worked to bring women together out of isolation into authentic community with genuine conversations about life and faith over shared meals. She serves as a volunteer mentor and blogger for the Military Spouse Advocacy Network, where she connects with new Navy spouses to guide them in their own journeys. Kara has also been a Registered Dietitian Nutritionist for over sixteen years, and can often be found reading cookbooks like juicy novels and is usually thinking about what's for dinner. She believes wholeheartedly in the mind-body-spirit connection in health and wellness, and is passionate about bringing that message to the military community. Connect with Kara on her blog at www.karaludlow.com.

Chapter Eight
MY RAINBOW CALLS ME MOMMY

MARLA BAUTISTA

THE TEARS ROLLED down my cheek as I whispered, "My perfect baby." The ultrasound pictured my growing boy, strong and without imperfection. I couldn't wait to meet the child I would come to call my rainbow baby. A rainbow baby is a name that identifies a healthy child born after a miscarriage or infant loss. The idea communicates the joy felt after a dark and gloomy season, representing beauty after a storm.

Less than a year earlier, I was diagnosed with fibroids, and I was told a successful pregnancy was not possible until they were removed. After two failed pregnancies, surgery, and a deployment, my rainbow was finally here.

My pregnancy was normal. I was initially plagued by morning sickness which soon gave way to a growing belly and round ligament pain. My craving for hot polish sausages might have been a little abnormal, but I thought, *who cares*. This was my opportunity to eat all the things I wanted without regret, and I did. At least, until heartburn became the dictator of my food intake. I enjoyed it—the pregnancy, not the heartburn. Feeling the baby move and grow was a dream come true.

My baby finally made his appearance after being a week overdue. I was induced, and eleven hours later, I was graced with his presence. My sweet Junior. His eyes, like silver marbles, twinkled under slivers of light that peered through the closed curtains of my hospital room. I was mesmerized as he ate from my breast. He was all mine.

After leaving the hospital, Junior taught me all about his little personality. How he loved to party at night and sleep peacefully during the day. Junior was a normal baby. He smiled, he cried, and he ate—a lot.

Breast milk was sort of his thing, until the introduction of real food. Pureed sweet potatoes became his new favorite. As he got older, his food preference didn't change. He didn't eat a wide variety of foods. But that didn't really concern me, because he was a chunky baby.

On Junior's first birthday, we were on an airplane heading to our new home in Germany. My husband received orders months earlier to live abroad. It didn't come as a surprise to us. We knew we couldn't remain at one location forever. As a matter of fact, we were excited. A new adventure awaited us across the pond.

Three days after moving to Germany, Junior began to walk without help. It was a bit overwhelming, seeing him in action. My baby was growing up right before my very eyes. Watching his little legs run up and down the hotel hallway brought me indescribable joy. A few months after transitioning into our new home, we noticed Junior was having some problems speaking. He began babbling like any other baby. Saying mama, dada, and other gibberish around nine months of age. But that was it. Those two words were the extent of his vocabulary.

By the time Junior was one-and-a-half, I was pregnant with my second child. It wasn't a planned pregnancy, but I was excited, nonetheless. Being pregnant and having a toddler was a struggle I was not prepared for. During Junior's 18-month check-up, the doctor asked developmental questions that were more difficult to answer than usual. "Does he verbally ask for the things he wants?"

I answered, "No."

"Does he make eye contact?"

"No."

"Does he engage with other children in play?"

"No."

My concern turned into worry as I wondered if I was doing a good job as his mother. Junior was my firstborn. I read to him before and after his birth. I showed him lots of pictures and sang nursery rhymes to him every day.

When I was told he had Autism Spectrum Disorder and Sensory Processing Disorder, it was something I couldn't comprehend. *What the heck was autism?* Although I was afraid of what the diagnosis meant for my son, in a way I was relieved to know the cause of his food adversity and speech delay.

Therapy soon took over our schedule, as we attended speech, occupational, and feeding therapies multiple days per week. I was tired. I was spread too thin. Being the wife of a soldier, I spent much of the parenting time alone.

Sometimes, I wondered if the hardships I faced were because of the things I did in the past. I made mistakes and more than a few bad choices. *Was this my punishment?* All of these thoughts created doubt and depression in me.

Eventually, I came to realize my son having autism was not

a punishment. It was a blessing in disguise. It was an opportunity to get him the extra help he needed to be successful in life. However, putting him in a place where he could receive a proper education proved more difficult than I'd imagined.

Junior didn't transition well, which caused him to have social anxiety and outbursts when interacting with new classmates. We tried medications. Some made him sleepy, some made him aggressive, some made him hungry, and some completely eliminated his entire personality. I felt defeated.

> **GOD'S WORD IS TRUE. LIVE FOR TODAY, LOVE FOR TODAY, BE GRATEFUL FOR WHAT YOU HAVE TODAY, AND YOU WILL BE BLESSED WITH A SOUND MIND.**

Every time we moved, a new doctor gave us a new medication to try. This pattern got old, quick. Finally, I made an important decision.

I chose to believe that Junior was okay. Yes, he has autism, but he is okay. He's perfect just the way he is. He still attends therapies and receives his education through special needs programs. But his prognosis is always improving.

Life after Junior's diagnosis has been difficult, but not unlivable. After a while, he began to progress and grow in ways I never thought were possible. I can only credit God for the faithfulness he's shown my family when we needed it the most. I spent days, weeks, and months worrying about my son's future. These feelings were something a woman of faith should not allow to penetrate her spirit.

Matthew 6:34 says, "Therefore do not worry about tomorrow, for tomorrow will worry about itself. Each day has enough trouble of its own."

God's Word is true. Live for today, love for today, be grateful for what you have today, and you will be blessed with a sound mind.

On the days when I struggle, I read Ephesians 4:2: *Be completely humble and gentle; be patient, bearing with one another in love.* I am blessed. The gift of his life reminds me daily of the blessings of God. Junior is my rainbow after the storm, bright and effervescent.

MARLA is the author of *My Thoughts Abandoned*, released in 2017. She has also written for and been featured in many national publications. However, her passion is giving to people in need. Marla is the founder of the Bautista Project Inc, a nonprofit organization that provides basic living essentials for homeless community members.

Chapter Nine
SACRIFICE

CHANDEE ULCH

I GAVE THE WAITRESS a look, daring her to interrupt our conversation. She quickly got the hint and walked past our table. Sitting with my daughter and her boyfriend in IHOP, I began to ask them questions about their relationship. I could tell things were moving too fast, considering they were only seventeen and eighteen. I wanted them to pause and consider the consequences of their choices, before they were faced with long-term repercussions.

"What does it mean to love someone?" I said.

"I think it is what you do for someone," he replied.

I looked at my daughter, waiting for her response.

"I agree with what he said. It is what you are willing to do for someone," said Shina.

I realized looking at love from the young enthusiastic eyes of teenagers, it would appear to be what you "do" for someone.

Looking back, when I said "I do" to my husband, it may have been my perspective of love as well. Time and the Lord have taught me a much different outlook.

Having a relationship that spans nearly two decades with my husband, I've learned that trying to decide what to share in a short moment isn't easy. I wondered: *Should I share with you the mistakes that taught us some hard lessons? Do I tell you about the accidental corrections we made by God's grace? Maybe, I should tell the stories of the highs and lows in our marriage. But my fear is no matter what I share, you will never get a full picture of "us."*

The story of "us" is quite a God-given, beautiful narrative. No one on earth would have put us together, but God did. Maybe the best place to start is at the beginning and time-lapse on fast-forward, to give you a decent view of this military marriage.

William is eighteen years older than me. He has been married before—to be exact, three other times. Although I hadn't married previously, I still came into this marriage with heartache and baggage.

He had the most beautiful ring made for me—a circle formed by dolphins, and in the center, three glistening diamonds. The day he handed me this ring, he said, "I never had a marriage where God was the center of it. I never want another marriage without God. This ring is to remind us, the Father, the Son, and the Holy Spirit are to always be in the center of us."

The day I married William, my "I do" wasn't just to him, it was to the Lord as well. It was a commitment I made to both. This constant reminder on my hand has carried me through some hard times.

Our marriage has endured tremendous joy and loss. We have seen the death of loved ones, our child, and five miscarriages. We have slept many nights apart, as long as twenty-four months when he was deployed, and adventured through ten moves within two countries and five states. We have experienced geo-baching twice ("Geo-Bach" is a slang term that means Geographical Bachelor). He lived in one state, while we lived in another state, for over a year. Needless to say, we have experienced a lot together.

How have we gotten through it all? It's not what we've done for each other—there's a deeper aspect to our commitment. Our willingness to sacrifice for one another is one of our secrets. Sacrifice is so much more than the act of doing.

First, I must mention the little ways we sacrifice. For instance, William accepts my hatred for making beds, and therefore, he does it every morning. I discovered he dislikes it when I squeeze the toothpaste from the middle, so to keep peace, I buy bottled toothpaste now. I know he doesn't like doing the dishes, so we handed the chore over to our kids (okay, it might have been a bonus for both of us). I know he sincerely dislikes vegetables, so I only push green beans, as I encourage him to eat at least one vegetable.

Then there are big sacrifices we've both made. When our son, Matthias, was born, William was called home from Iraq. After they let Matthias out of the Neonatal Intensive Care Unit, the military sent William back. The same day he was returning to a war zone, our son ended up on a ventilator. My daughter, sick with pneumonia, had to go to another state with her grandparents.

I sat in the Pediatric Intensive Care Unit (PICU) with my son, while a machine breathed for him. My daughter, sick without her mama, caused a deep ache in my heart. Both of these crises made me desperately want William home again.

The doctors continually asked if I wanted to call my husband back. My heart did, but my duty knew he was under so much stress of his own. I was concerned an international trip wasn't in his best interest. I told them "no," not unless they knew our son Matthias wasn't going to get better.

During that highly emotional period, I had to remember it wasn't about what I wanted, it was about what was best for William's safety and health. I wanted him to keep his mind on his job so he could return home alive. I had to think long-term. It was a sacrifice, sitting in a room alone, watching machines ding and buzz for my baby. I was heartbroken, listening to my daughter on the phone sick. The Christmas of 2006 came and went while William was separated from us, thousands of miles away. I shed tears daily.

I KNEW I HAD TO CONVEY LOVE DEMONSTRATED THROUGH SACRIFICE, AND IT WASN'T GOING TO BE EASY.

As the new year in 2007 arrived, the doctors decided to call William back from Iraq again. They were considering open-heart surgery for Matthias, and they wanted him in the states. William walked into the PICU in his uniform, strong and stern, tired, and stressed. He kissed me and went straight to his son. As he put his hands on our boy's tiny body, you could see the heart monitor rise. Matthias knew his daddy was there.

Over the next few weeks, the doctors, William, and I, decided open-heart surgery wasn't necessary. Matthias eventually came off the ventilator, and he went home with an apnea monitor. He used it until he was almost four years old.

For a third time, William flew back to Iraq to complete his tour. Standing in the airport, watching our five-year-old girl cry, as I held our three-month-old son, I fought to show strength. I knew in that moment, our marriage wasn't going to be about what we do for each other, it was going to be about how we chose to sacrifice for each other.

Flash forward to IHOP, where I faced my beautiful daughter who believed she fully understood love. I knew I had to convey love demonstrated through sacrifice, and it wasn't going to be easy. But my daughter and her boyfriend needed to comprehend the true power of love. The power in what they, as individuals, were willing to give up for one another. I wanted them to ponder this question, "What did Jesus do to show the world how much He truly loved us?"

Yes, Jesus did many things. He raised people from the dead. He cast out demons. He healed the sick. He turned water into wine. All of it was wonderful. But, His real love, His greatest love, was shown in His sacrifice. When He chose to lay down His life for us. When He willingly crawled onto the cross, beaten and bleeding, suffering our punishment, when He gave up everything for us. That was the moment His love was truly demonstrated. True love is a sacrifice.

Throughout our marriage, the one thing I know for certain is this—the sacrifice William and I choose daily is the greatest act of love we can give each other. If this is the only lesson I ever teach my children, I pray they know it is a lesson God first taught and gave to us. Love isn't what you do, it's what you release, especially when it's hard.

THIS SHORT bio can never really convey the diverse of dimensions of who Chandee is, however, if you know nothing about her, know this; She loves deeply and is fiercely loyal. Her confidence comes from Christ, although she struggles with fear too. Stubborn and sarcastic with a bit of a sadistic sense of humor, she'll make you smile. Her closet companies are her family. Married to William for almost twenty years, now, has earned her the title of a "seasoned military spouse". Translation; they have been doing this military life a long darn time. Most people don't realize in the military world that what you set out as your career, rarely is what you get to do. Explaining why her current resume looks like a jigsaw puzzle; she's worked in the medical field.

She graduated from Columbia International University with a degree in Bible, Intercultural Studies and Teaching English as a Second Language. She taught internationally and contracted with the military. Chandee also attended The Art Institute of Charlotte where she focused on photography and videography. She's an author, public speaker, and producer. In the midst of all this, they have been blessed with two wonderful children. Shina is a ray of sunshine and Matthias is strong little man. As she shares her life stories with the world her desire to be raw with the challenges of life, while praising God along the way. She never holds back, not in her joys nor struggles with military life, loss, family, or raising children. She longs to share all God is teaching her through the storms of life, corrections, and blessings. She needs her testimony to make a Heavenly difference.

Chapter Ten
HOME IS WHERE THE MARINE CORPS SENDS YOU

JOLYNN LEE

THROUGHOUT OUR TIME in the military, we had a sign that hung as you entered our home. It stated, "Home is where the Marine Corps sends you."

So much truth captured in eight little words. But even more profound and honest is the statement, "Home is where the heart is."

For so many of us living this military life, home is a loaded, four-letter word. It can mean the physical place you reside, the loving refuge you left behind, or the better half of you located somewhere other than where you are physically located. I learned early on, "Home" was the refuge I created, regardless of the location.

We have the great blessing of four lovely children, three of whom are adults and married with families of their own. I often tell fellow military spouses who worry this lifestyle will ruin their kids not to fret too much.

Three of our children spent their entire lives moving with their dad's military career. Two of them married Marines, and one joined the Corps himself. So, it can't be that bad of a gig. Somehow, despite the distance and permanent change of station orders that can arrive at random, we stay connected and interwoven in each other's lives in an almost uncanny way.

At one point during our military journey, my daughters and I all lived on the same base. It was during this rotation, that our son ended up stationed at the same base as well, living in the barracks. My neighbors used to comment "How do you get all your adult children to WANT to come home so often?"

We gathered every Sunday after church for a family dinner and played whatever physical game the season rated outside. We got together for holidays, birthdays, and any random event that gave us the opportunity. The kids brought their friends, and we lived by the motto, "The more the merrier."

My husband once sat in a meeting with the Chief of Staff and several higher-ranking personnel and was asked, somewhat accusatorially, why there were so many cars at our home with so many differing rank structures. His reply, "They are all my family." Stares of disbelief and shock followed. The staff meeting immediately shifted from the business at hand to questions regarding how he managed to keep everyone together with the push and pull of military life.

I would love to say we have a secret formula for togetherness, or a magic recipe that draws us all to the dinner table in unity, but the truth of the matter is, we are simply intentional about relationship. We know that love takes work and investment, and we are very blessed to not just love one another, but to also like one another as well.

I didn't grow up in the military lifestyle, my dad was a civilian. But if you looked at my school transcript you might wonder. I literally moved every two years until high school. My dad was in college athletics. And like the military, there was always a change at hand that came at the most unexpected, and often inopportune, time.

I lived away from all my relatives my whole life. And while I considered Kentucky to be my home, I only lived there for a few months when I was first born. We returned again when my dad worked at the University of Louisville for a season.

Every vacation my parents took was spent driving to Kentucky from whatever region of the United States we currently lived. All holidays were spent trekking back to see the relatives. It was what we did, what we wanted to do—even though it was exhausting and costly (both with time and money).

> **I LEARNED THAT MAINTAINING RELATIONSHIPS ACROSS THE MILES TAKES EFFORT, CREATIVITY, CONSISTENCY AND INTENTIONALITY.**

Summers were often our moving season, and occasionally I stayed with my grandparents in Kentucky while my parents made the geographical transition and house-hunted. It was easier for us all that way. I valued those moments with my relatives. It gave me an appreciation for family that I think can be overlooked when you grow up in the same place with the same people your whole life.

When I married into the military at eighteen and started my own geographical transitioning, I gained insight from my long-distance family relationships. I learned that maintaining relationships across the miles takes effort, creativity, consistency and intentionality. My parents had indirectly taught me how to do this on our many trips home as I was growing up. But now, it was exemplified in a new way by their actions with my little family.

My granny and Dad always had a motto, "Make memories!" My dad demonstrated that motto throughout the years with my kids by traveling to see us every chance he got, so he could be a part of their daily lives. He and his wife didn't just hit the highlights with the holidays, they came for soccer tournaments, class field trips, and Grandparent's Day at the kids' schools. My dad didn't just travel himself, he made the effort to bring his mom (Granny) and his sister as often as he could.

I can honestly say, there is not a place we have been stationed that my dad has not visited, usually within the first month of our transition. (My husband thinks it is because my dad wanted to ensure we were living in decent quarters and was checking up on us.) Whatever the reason, that effort and consistency taught my children they were valued, and that no matter where we might be physically located, their grandparents would be present. Their effort during those earlier years laid the groundwork for me with my own family. We consistently lived to "make memories" with each other, because we tried to maintain a value for the time we had together, knowing it was measured and often limited.

As my kids got older and became more engaged and involved in life and friends, we made sure to be creative in cultivating connections within our direct family unit. My husband and I established "Amnesty Day" when our kids were in middle/high school. They could share anything and everything going on in their lives with no fear of repercussion. No punishment would be issued, and no rule changes would be implemented as a result of confiding. It was an exercise in trust. They learned to trust us to honor our word and be parents with whom they could share openly and honestly. We learned to trust their desire to come clean with whatever they might be harboring internally. (Jeff and I also used this as an avenue to have our eyes and ears opened to things we may have missed on the parenting front.)

I learned from my geographically distant relatives that consistency matters in relationship building. My grandmother called every weekend without fail. I could expect a phone call at some point on Sunday afternoon, and I was required to give her a weekly update on our lives, as well as to listen to her report on the goings-on back home in Kentucky. I could count on her. She was reliable and faithful in her commitment to me and my family. Relationships take that kind of effort, the kind that is faithful and painstaking, but dependable and secure. Basically, you should be so consistent in your reliability of relationship that it is almost boring.

Above all, remember that establishing a solid home front on the go does not happen by accident. I have preached to my kids their whole lives, "You reap what you sow."

(Kentucky was a farming community, so I use farm metaphors.) If you want a crop of wheat you have to plant wheat. If you want to grow corn you have to plant corn. If you want strong family connections and ties, then you'd better plant strong and healthy family relationship seeds.

Where your time, effort, and energy go, your heart will follow. So, if you want connections, if you want relationship, if you want family, then you have to plant those seeds of relationship early. When you establish healthy communication and trust, you make memories from which to water your love when you're apart or in times of turmoil. You guard against any weeds that try to crowd in and steal away the harvest of family connection. It is hard work, and it can be dirty work, but family is worth the effort always!

But military life also taught me that family can be more

than those to whom we are blood related. Family is also born in the midst of life's shared journey. We have been fortunate to encounter friends in this military life who are now family. Those relationships were birthed out of the blood, sweat, and tears of shared experience. As much as I love my relatives back home, they don't truly understand what it means to watch for a glimpse of news when a loved one is at war. Fearing the ringing phone or chiming doorbell after a reported military accident or action is tough. Shared history bonds hearts in a powerful way. And for those of us in this military lifestyle, family becomes a more inclusive, broader-reaching terminology that defines not just who we are, but what we have experienced. It's what we do, how we live, and how we survive and thrive within the military community.

My children are now a part of this military lifestyle, on their own, by their own design. And they carry with them the legacy with which they were raised—the traditions, the nuances of relationship, the memories, both good and bad. But they have already started forming their extended family relationships—filled with friends who have supported them during deployments, overseas births, marriage ups and downs, and through moves and transitions.

I am thankful to see them so open and willing to cultivate those connections, to open their hearts, families, and homes to people, and to step into those deep and lasting relationships. I know it will make them stronger. It will make this lifestyle so much more enjoyable. And their lives will be richer for the sharing. To those of us who live this roller coaster life of the military, family means everything and so much more.

JOLYNN LEE is a speaker, writer, mentor, and military family advocate. She was married to the Marine Corps for 30 years, while her husband served on active duty. She now proudly wears the title of

Marine mom and Marine mother-in-law. She is the mother of five children (ages 29, 27, 25, 12 and 10) and grandmother to seven grand-blessings. Jolynn and her husband work hard to make memories with their children and grandchildren and do not take their moments of combined family fellowship for granted. They love to play family football at Thanksgiving, and always have a Christmas Day nerf war. They are as committed to their faith, family, and friends as they are winning the family games, with an intensity and focus that does not back down.

Jolynn supports her military community and utilizes her graduate degree in counseling from Liberty University by volunteering with multiple non-profit organizations. She and her husband are site leaders for REBOOT Combat Recovery – Camp Lejeune, a faith-based trauma recovery program open to all active duty personnel, veterans, and their families. She is also the Community Development Team Lead for Planting Roots: Strength to Thrive in Military Life, a ministry for military women and wives. In addition, Jolynn was elected President of the Camp Lejeune Leadership Seminar for 2020. After 30 years of military marriage, Jolynn was honored to have served as the 2018-Armed Force Insurance Marine Corps Spouse of the Year. That 2018 experience helped reaffirm her belief that we are #strongertogether. You can learn more about Jolynn, or follow her writing on her website, www.jolynnlee.com, where she hosts "Starfish Talks" and shares stories of faith and hope that #reachjustone.

Part Three

FRIENDS THAT BECOME FAMILY: RELATIONSHIPS AND COMMUNITY

Chapter Eleven
HOW A RED TENT BECAME A PLACE FOR SOUL FOOD

AJ SMIT

STONE SOUP SOUNDS inedible. But this concept from a children's story by the same name implies a cooperative and collaborative undertaking that brings people together.

In the story, everyone from the village brings a little bit of food to the community pot—roots or vegetables they have left over, chicken bones for broth, and one-half of a clove of garlic. When mixed together it creates a delicious stew the village enjoys together, uniting them in a satisfying communal meal.

The same thing happens in a Red Tent gathering. But instead of vegetables for soup, we bring our stories. As military spouses, Tent has created a grounding place where we share stories to create a sacred space yielding food for our souls. Community is oft-touted as grabbing some friends and going out for coffee, getting your nails done, or seeing a movie. But *true* community is cultivated in the sharing of stories and life experiences.

Red Tent is a gathering of women once a month to talk about what it means to be an embodied woman in this world. We sing songs, share stories, dance, and rest. In each Tent gathering, a woman shares her womanhood story. Their story could be anything—the birth of a child, a miscarriage, a rape, their first period, or how their journey has been impacted by the women they have known. There have been tears, laughter, silence, and shouting. These stories are sacred. We come together to hear stories.

We've often been taught to fear sharing with others.

Some stories make us freeze. We are told, "It was your fault," or "You should have known." We have experienced an onslaught of advice after sharing a secret we hoped would be held gently.

There's a space in Tent for pain and joy—not an either/or situation. We listen with soft hearts, open hands, and silent lips. And we find, again and again, in this sacred space we create, the power of women healing women.

As women, we learn at an early age the way to serve is to pour endlessly from our cup into the cups of those who are not interested in nourishing us. In a true community, like a Red Tent, women can pour into the communal bowl of listening, sharing, and being present. And in doing so, we ourselves are nourished. To create a true community of military spouses, whether it is a Red Tent or not, we must create a stone soup of all our best and worst experiences—our dreams, our heartbreak, our desires, our fears of PCS news, and our feelings about our spouses going abroad.

These stories mix to bring a unique flavor to each gathering—the bitter bay leaves of grief, mixed with the sturdy carrots of forging through a hard day, and a small broken leek of unexpected news—seasoned with the joy of someone finding a new job. Each participant in the community gently adds their story to the pot. Some days, women choose to just be mindful in the space, unable to share. They stir the pot with their presence. Occasionally, all one has to offer is the bones of what is left of them from that day, week, or year. Those who come knowing that restoration happens in community, create the broth of trust. All are welcome in our stone soup of stories.

In a Red Tent, there is no silent fear or shame. Participants' cups are emptied out in front of each other—our petty indignation, our secret questions, our piteous laments, and our fiercest wishes. We hear each other's fears and hopes—and we see ourselves in them. We tell each other we are not alone in these thoughts. Sharing our burdens traditionally results in receiving advice or being "fixed" or "helped." However, in Red Tent, we find that simply listening and saying, "I see you. You can pour here in our bowl. You don't have to keep it all in your cup." These words provide a balm of peace-giving grace.

WE LISTEN WITH SOFT HEARTS, OPEN HANDS, AND SILENT LIPS.

At the end of a Red Tent evening, once everyone has poured their stories in, we find something remarkable. We each have a fuller cup than what we came in with. Our cups are no longer a display of female martyrdom—whose cup is emptiest, who is most exhausted, who is busiest, or who has won the Misery Olympics.

No. The end of a Red Tent brings an awareness of who we are, who we were created to be. What our cups look like is an acknowledgment of the journeys we have been on, and together we sip our well-deserved stone soup. A few cups are bright and shiny, others dull from use. Many have tiny chips with gold lining, evidence of healing God has done in us. They all hold the same soup.

At the end of the evening, we do a Red Thread ceremony. Red Thread represents our connection to each other. We stand in a circle and wrap crimson yarn around our wrists, reciting our matriarchal lineage as we do so. We wrap the thread, then we pass it on, wrap the thread, then pass on again. We pass the thread as we passed our stories. When finished, a complete red circle of thread represents the connectedness of our community. Though this may seem a bit much to some, remember, rituals are tangible displays of our deepest intentions. To close the Red Tent, we sing a simple song together. Our bodies sway, our eyes are closed, and we know: This. Is. Good. Here, we are safe and held. Here, our triumphs, our fears, our broken dreams, and our secret questions are all wanted and welcome.

You may believe an empty cup is a virtue, that you have to be exhausted to be a "good woman." Or your cup may already be full—full of fear, self-loathing, guilt, or shame. However, in Red Tent, when we pour our stories together, heavy secrets become stories we can process. And shame withers in the light of shared experience.

Pouring out your story requires boldness, to be sure. So does admitting you feel empty. The truth is, none of us have enough for a whole soup—we need each other. We need people. We need a community that can hold space for us and identify with our stories. Stone soup is not simply a children's story about sharing. It is a community-building approach. Though none of us are whole, in sharing, we create a nourishing place of belonging for all. My dream is for everyone to find a place they can gather and make stone soup of their stories.

AJ is the owner and founder of *In Joy Productions*. As a military spouse living in Germany, she decided to create her own Red Tent using her theatre degree, enthusiasm for storytelling, and love of bringing people together. Since then, she has held sacred spaces for women to flourish through Red Tents, retreats, and soul art workshops both internationally and in the United States. With her traveling red tent and Creative Soul Conversations, she now facilitates these conversations in engaging ways for people to weave curiosity and creativity into their lives and businesses. Living in San Antonio, Texas, with her husband Jeremy, two pups, and a bucketful of glitter for emergencies, Aj usually has a book or paintbrush in hand, exploring how to better love God, love people, and live intentionally. She is a co-host of the "Crushin' It" podcast and writes for *Gems Magazine*, *Military Spouse Magazine*, The Agenda (period), and MilSpoCo.com. To cultivate your joy, or join an online or in-person Red Tent, you can find her at @MermaidHarmony and @InJoyProductions on Facebook and Instagram. She also has a Facebook group *Embodied In Joy* you can join, or check out her website at www.AjSmit.com

Chapter Twelve
STRONGER TOGETHER

SHERRY EIFLER

WHO CAN I trust? Where can I turn for help?

Those questions cross my mind with every move or military Permanent Change of Station (PCS). As an Army wife, I've moved sixteen times, averaging a move every two years. Each move has proven a life-changing transition full of emotional farewells and exhausting questions about future acceptance or rejection.

Sometimes, I think about just sticking to myself, it's too exhausting to get involved and make new friends, it would be easier that way. Of course, I know the opposite is true. Sticking to myself has never worked for me, that mindset only leads to the deadly "I" word—Isolation. And I'm not the only one who understands the danger.

Studies have "found that loneliness and social isolation are twice as harmful to physical and mental health as obesity" (*Perspectives on Psychological Science*, Vol. 10, No. 2, 2015). We were created for community—we are not meant to do life on our own. Isolation happens when we pull inward and stop reaching out.

A strong woman is not one who insists on flying solo. A strong woman asks, creates, and invests in a community around her, encouraging others to share the load. She fills in the gaps with each person's talents and abilities. Doing life together creates a greater opportunity to experience living in a more meaningful way, full of authentic connection.

Stronger together is a mindset that locks out isolation. Ecclesiastes 4:9-12 reminds us that, "Two are better than one, because they have a good return for their labor: . . . one falls . . . one helps the other up . . . ."

Unfortunately, women mask isolation masterfully from themselves and others, but only for so long. Eventually, the mask begins to crack from pressures, and reality is seen when we look in the mirror, or others take notice. When the truth becomes evident, we feel alone and weak.

During a deployment, while living overseas, a young mother fell into isolation as she navigated an unfamiliar environment. She was torn by the loss of a family member an ocean away.

This woman tried to hide the cracks she knew were showing. Time and again, she neglected to accept the offers of other wives, who invited her to join them. Perhaps she did not want to appear weak and needy, or maybe it was too scary to let someone see the full scope of her reality.

One day, her neighbor knocked on her door with fresh flowers in hand. But in that moment, the sweet mother's mask was slipping. The truth was exposed, when she couldn't hide her desperate need any longer.

The young woman's home was in utter disarray, and her

screaming toddler reinforced the fact that she was a barely-making-it mother. I understood.

Despite the heartbreaking reality of the situation, the memory warms my heart, because what I remember most vividly is seeing trust form in this precious young mother's eyes. She simply needed a safe place to go.

Countless times, I've found myself looking for a trustworthy and safe place. Even in a room full of people, I have felt completely alone. Trying to control perception with my carefully placed mask, I've hoped to prevent close contact, in case someone might see my cracks, flaws, and genuine frailty. Though the question always nags *Where can I turn and still keep my mask?* The masquerade is exhausting, isolating, and comfortable, all at the same time.

> **COUNTLESS TIMES, I'VE FOUND MYSELF LOOKING FOR A TRUSTWORTHY AND SAFE PLACE.**

Life has a way of pushing us out from behind our masks, forcing us to choose between continued isolation and an authentic community. We can only get so far on our own. I've learned, little by little with each military move, that prayer and community provide the answer to my need for strength and encouragement.

As my family grew through the years, we started praying at each whisper of a Permanent Change Station. Over time, our prayers focused more on our next set of trusted friends and our faith community, and less about our next physical home. We came to understand strength together, and home is where the Army sends us.

The Lord is faithful and has answered our prayers with each PCS. In our first overseas move as a family, my husband was scheduled for deployment while he was serving as a commander. As a leader's wife, the questions of "who can be trusted" and "where can I turn," took on new meaning, while I sought authentic community. So, the prayerful search began, and God sent Heather to me.

After a few months of watching our children play together, enjoying spontaneous adventures, and sharing inner-heart secrets, we planned a fun day that began with a last-minute detour—a quick ultrasound stop. When my name was called, I left my friend in the waiting room with our combined five children. The kids bubbled with excitement, waiting to go to a new indoor kid zone.

My anticipation for the day was interrupted when the ultrasound tech said, "Oh. I will be right back."

As I stumbled numbly from the exam room, my mind raced with questions. *Am I going to put on a mask to cover the fear rising in me or am I going to trust Heather?* I decided to remove the mask. I reached out.

What followed was weeks of living in the abyss of the unknown. I left the hospital with new knowledge—I had lesions on my liver. I waited for the CT scans to come back, but they revealed no definitive results. Heather stood by me, as I waited to tell my husband, who was away training his unit for war. In private, Heather saw behind my mask, as I shook with the fear of uncertainty and searched for words and strength in prayer. God and my friend repeatedly helped me face my children with peace.

A diagnosis, followed by emergency surgery in a German hospital scheduled around my husband's brief return, led to months of recovery. I could have chosen to screw on my emotional mask, refusing to let Heather see my struggle and pain. However, if I had chosen the mask, I would have been left in isolation and my family would have suffered from the backlash of an unstable wife and mother. Thankfully, Heather was my closest confidant during that tough time, but not my only help.

I was blessed beyond measure by friends the Lord sent to walk alongside my family. My friends filled in the gaps and allowed me to gain my strength. When my soldier and his unit left for war, because of those who were lifting me up, he could stand with confidence, knowing his family was surrounded by a unified community. We would receive support while he was gone.

The deadly "I" word, Isolation, could have stolen my life if I had chosen the mask over the truth of transparency—providing real strength. Likewise, isolation could have diminished the life of a sweet young mother, if she hadn't bravely allowed her neighbor to show her care and gently step into the darkness of her isolation. The gentle light of hope shines when we do life together.

Life is messy because we are imperfect humans. But starting with ourselves makes us trustworthy and a safe place for others to turn to. We find we are not alone when we are in need. A stronger together mindset defeats the isolation mindset every time. Life beyond the mask is never something to fear. Uncovering is the secret to finding people—people we can count on, people we can lean on. These are the gifts we should gladly receive and pass on when we can. This is true community.

SHERRY EIFLER is a former soldier turned devoted Army wife and mom. She makes her home wherever the Army sends her husband of 25 years, Brian. Together they embrace the adventure of military life with their three amazing children and their faithful pup, Sol. The threads of faith, family, and friendship run through all that Sherry does. She is a recognized author, speaker, and transformation consultant. She is best known for her use of a multi-faceted approach to launch her clients to live their purpose and power. As the CEO of

R Connection Point, she continues to provide a personal approach to her design and delivery as a speaker and executive coach. She speaks from the heart, each event is engaging and professionally enhanced through her kaleidoscope of experiences, certifications, and talents as a business owner, author, and Executive Director with The John Maxwell Team. Sherry continues to share her faith journey through her Bible study *Royal Reflections- The Making of a Warrior Princess*. You can learn more at www.SherryEifler.com or connect with her at www.RConnectionPoint.com.

Chapter Thirteen
GRIEVING BROKEN THINGS

MEGAN HARLESS

EVERY YEAR, UP to 450,000 service members and their families will embark on a Permanent Change of Station (PCS). Their homes and all their belongings will be packed into cardboard boxes by complete strangers, loaded onto big semi-trucks, and driven to a new home thousands of miles away. They will repeat this process every 12-36 months until they decide their time in the military is complete. In retrospect, an average person will move eleven times in their entire lifetime, a military family will easily exceed that within a 20-year military career.

That means from every one to three years, a military family starts all over: new location, new jobs, new schools, new doctors, new home, and new community. The only constant they have in their lives are each other and their material household goods arriving in the moving truck. Wherever the military may send them, they will have the comfort of the same worn-down couch, kitchen table, and the end tables that have been painted multiple times to fit the new color scheme of each new house.

They will spend days purging the home of unwanted and unneeded things and prepacking their most important items. Time is spent deciding what will go in the suitcase and what can go on the truck. Crews from the moving company will come and pack up everything, while leaving a trail of unpackable items such as batteries, lightbulbs, and candles. The day will come where everything is then loaded onto a large truck, and the place that felt like home for the last few years will then become empty. A cold house will take its place in your heart with the memories made there.

When our household goods show up at the receiving location, it is no surprise to find some items scratched, dented, or broken into pieces. We expect there will be damage that happens during the transit of our possessions. There is an unspeakable expectation that some things may show up completely damaged. And when it does, we will repaint the end table again, get a new knob for a dresser, or add a felt pad to the bottom in order to make the wobbly chair stable again. Other times, we'll figure out how to repurpose the old dresser into a new TV stand, because the drawers showed up in multiple pieces, or how to turn broken kitchen chairs into patio stools.

However, there are times when some things show up so damaged they cannot be salvaged, or are even missing. Moving companies will tell families to file reimbursement claims. But there are times when money just cannot replace the things that get lost or broken beyond repair. Some items are more than just items—they are our constants in life, they are our memories.

The kitchen table is not just a kitchen table. It is the table where other spouses came and had Thanksgiving dinner with us when our husbands were deployed. It is the table where we invited the soldiers living in the barracks to come have Christmas dinner with us so they wouldn't be alone. It's the gathering place where my children had their first solid foods, where school projects were assembled, and crafts were made for holidays.

It may seem like an old worn out sewing machine and table, but to me it is more than that. It is the sewing machine my grandmother taught me to sew on. I sat next to her and gently guided the fabric straight through the needle as she controlled the speed. It then became the same sewing machine handed on to me after her passing, where I started teaching my own daughter to sew in the same fashion, resting her hands on mine to guide the fabric through.

The small box not checked off the inventory, missing from our truck, is the box that contained china and crystal from our wedding, my grandma's handwritten recipes, and pictures from my childhood. Things that should have moved with us but didn't fit in the suitcases to move across the ocean. It was my favorite piece of furniture, the bookshelf my grandfather built that didn't arrive—things that helped us hold on to those memories, the places we have lived and visited. The stories of each child being born in a different state are contained in things that cannot be replaced with money from a claim.

In these moments, we grieve the loss of things that filled our houses and minds. The objects that would have helped to make this new space feel more like a home. The items that make the adjustment from one location to another smoother for our children. We grieve the loss of possessions that linked us to our memories and made the cold, empty house into our new family home.

It is not the first time our treasured belongings have shown up shattered into pieces, and it won't be the last. We will replace the table split in half, reupholster the chair with the ripped fabric seat, and do our best to fix the shelves, so they can last just a little bit longer before we need to buy new ones. When the items show up missing all together, we'll do our best to explain to our children that their toy box can be replaced with a better one. We will tell ourselves that it is just stuff. It is simply wood, fabric, pieces of metal, nails and screws.

As America continues to call our service members to service and move us around the world where needed, we will go. We will continue to pack up our homes, leave our communities, leave our newfound comfort, and go where the military says our spouses are needed. We will cross our fingers, make a wish, and pray everything shows up and the damage is minimal. And when it doesn't, when our possessions are shattered or missing, we'll take a moment and grieve the loss of our material goods. We'll grieve the loss of those items which were a constant in this ever-changing military life, and then we'll move on. This is simply what we are called to do.

IN THESE MOMENTS, WE GRIEVE THE LOSS OF THINGS THAT FILLED OUR HOUSES AND MINDS.

While we continue to answer the call to God's service, we take hope in knowing what Matthew 6:19-20 tells us: *"Don't store up treasures here on earth, where moths eat them and rust destroys them, and where thieves break in and steal. Store your treasures in heaven where moths and rust cannot destroy and thieves do not break in and steal."*

When that box of broken china shows up, and I grieve the memory of tea parties with my grandmother, I will take hope in knowing that in the end, our material possessions cannot come with us to the other side. I find comfort in knowing that reuniting with my grandmother in a place far better is what matters most.

When you see that military family roll down your street with their moving truck in tow, show compassion. When you see that family looking like they are about to give everything up and cry, as a pile of broken furniture sits on their lawn, provide the comfort they may need. Remind them that even with the physical item gone or ruined, their memories will continue. What an amazing opportunity your friendship holds—you could help them make new memories and share some encouragement. After all, Heaven is our home—not here—but for now, we're here together.

(See Megan Harless's bio in Chapter Three)

Chapter Fourteen
MY VILLAGE. OUR VILLAGE.

MARLA BAUTISTA

WE'VE ALL SEEN it. The smiling military family matched in their patriotic colors and waving their American flags.

While the media gets the comradery and sense of pride correct, there is a deeper side to this military life. One where a small community built by circumstance turns into a family, or a group of strangers from different backgrounds become sisters. The women I've met know it takes a village to survive. Loneliness and isolation are the silent killers in our community, but sharing in fellowship allows us to struggle through, and fall forward together in victory. This is military life, and this is my story.

Growing up was traumatic for me. My parents died before I was ten years old. I suffered abuse by someone I trusted. I was left broken and confused. There was no one I could confide in, and nowhere I could go. As a child, I was used to trauma and loneliness.

However, I never thought I'd have to experience it as a military wife. Of course, I didn't think being married to a soldier would be easy. But watching the men and women who volunteered their lives for the sake of mine, only to be injured or left in despair, is something I was not prepared for.

After meeting and falling head over heels for a guy I barely knew, we jumped the broom and exchanged vows. My husband and I were married after knowing each other for only thirty short days. As crazy as it sounds, it's not uncommon for military members to marry young or swiftly. We were young and reckless, so to speak. We soon learned that the military spouse journey is not for the faint of heart. You never know where military life will take you, or your spouse, for that matter. One day, we were living in marital bliss, cuddled under a blanket watching movies as a snowstorm created a winter wonderland outside of our windows. The next day, we were experiencing heartbreak and fear as deployment loomed.

Within the first year of our marriage, my husband was headed to war, and I was left behind. Living on an island in my early twenties, I felt isolated. I didn't know anyone. Moving away from family months before and suffering a miscarriage only weeks prior to deployment was devastating. I was living with a huge void. My spirit was weary. I needed something or someone to help me get by. I quickly learned an idle mind is truly the devil's playground. Feelings of resentment, jealousy, and anger became my norm. I needed support from someone, somewhere.

As the months grew long, I struggled to find peace. I had good days, but they were overshadowed by the constant anxiety of hoping my husband was still alive. This proved different from the images of military families you see on television.

What people don't see are the injuries, both physical and mental, suffered by our service members. We face broken families, addictions, and loneliness time and time again.

While my husband was gone, the thoughts that went through my head would make anyone go insane. *Why hasn't he called me today? Is he still alive? Is today the day the Chaplain is going to ring my doorbell?* These recurring thoughts plagued me. They made me sick.

I began to suffer physically from the stress I endured. I couldn't eat. I couldn't sleep. I was no longer my strong, independent self. I didn't understand why things were so hard. Then, I recalled a Bible verse embedded in me: *Finally, my brethren, be strong in the Lord, and in the power of his might. Put on the whole armor of God, that ye may be able to stand against the wiles of the devil* (Ephesians Chapter 6: 10-11 KJV).

With a little encouragement from my military sisters, I began to immerse myself in the Bible and going to church. Fasting, praying, and speaking positivity into my life helped change my outlook. My focus began to improve. I admit, some days were easier than others.

After a while, I started taking classes in team building, family readiness, and anything else that would help me settle into and embrace this new life of mine. I wanted to know everything there was to know about military life, and what I could do to make the best of it.

I eventually met other women like me. Struggling through deployment, hour by hour, and trying to make the best of our current circumstance. Before I knew it, these women were my village, and I was a part of theirs. We spent our days volunteering, and the nights binge-watching the television show, *Army Wives*. This was our new normal, our family far from home, forged by our spouses' military service. The laughter, tears, and even the arguments are what kept our bond strong. We prepared holiday meals for our unit and wrapped presents to fundraise, in order to provide a happy holiday season for our soldiers at war.

Volunteering within the military community helped me survive deployment. I loved assisting people, empowering communities, and strengthening organizations. This was my purpose, being a selfless servant. Volunteering as a unit family readiness group leader was a way to help keep military families informed and provided opportunities to build relationships among them. I organized potlucks and family fun events. It was a lot of work, but I had my village, and they had my back. Together, we experienced everything from the births of our babies, to the deaths of some of our service members. This life was tough. But through it all, we grew resilient. Facing each day, wearing the armor of God. That's the only way we survived.

We reminded each other of what strength and courage looked like. They were my friends who became my sisters. As a military family, we took pleasure in sharing meals and sending care packages to our troops. When times were tough, we relied on each other for reassurance and guidance.

Volunteering within the military community was great, but I wanted to do more. I wanted to change lives. I began using my gift of communication to help tell the stories of the voiceless. Spending time learning about the needs of our military families was eye opening. We had so much in common. Even though it seemed like we were vastly different, we struggled with many of the same things, like loneliness, hurt, and guilt. I knew encouragement was needed, not lofty prayers or glossed over Bible studies. We needed healing and the power to overcome our daily fears. We took up intermittent fasting, and we prayed for each other by name. We took prayer seriously, becoming intentional to know each other's lives well enough to be specific with our prayers. We fell on bended knee to ask God to meet our needs for love, joy, and peace.

Months went by, and finally, the light at the end of the deployment tunnel was quickly approaching. As we anxiously awaited the return of our soldiers, we also prepared for the separation of our village. Sadly, our time at any one duty station is short—maybe two or three years—in that time, we share highs and lows. We grieved and we rejoiced. But through it all, we had each other. A sense of community is what kept us going, when nothing else did. The closeness we once knew was coming to an end.

> **WE REMINDED EACH OTHER OF WHAT STRENGTH AND COURAGE LOOKED LIKE.**

We were now embracing our new normal of caring for our physically, mentally, and emotionally wounded soldiers. Helping them heal as we tried to mask our concerns.

My husband struggled. The nightmares, the weeping—it took a toll on us. Our marriage was in trouble. I needed my village. What got me through the hard times? Remembering the good times. Those late-night conversations with my friends helped me cope during lonely nights. Later, those same conservations reminded me of my resilience, and strengthened me yet again.

I've learned no matter where you are, you can have a village. You just have to be present. Love and support one another, especially in hard times. Our rainbow shines brighter when all the colors are present. In the military, a soldier's strength is only as strong as his or her battle buddy's. This, too, rings true for spouses. I am only as strong as my village—the mission is ours.

(See Maria Bautista's bio in Chapter Eight)

Chapter Fifteen
YOU ARE YOUR CIRCLE

KENNITA WILLIAMS

SURROUNDING YOURSELF WITH the right people is as important as eating the right foods. The people around you have a great impact on your life. Just like food, if you make bad choices, you will get unfavorable results. With this in mind, you must carefully select the people you spend your time with.

When selecting each person, ask yourself:

Does this person bring value to my life?
Will a relationship with this person evoke healthy growth?
How does this person add to my development?

The goal is to seek out a circle of friends who enrich your life by providing positivity, happiness, inspiration, and forward growth.

The late entrepreneur and author Jim Rohn put it simply, yet powerfully, when he said, "You are the average of the five people you spend most of your time with."

Be mindful of your circle. It's a fact of life that some people hold us back, while others propel us forward. For instance, you can't hang out with negative people and expect to have a positive life. If your goal is to be a spiritual warrior, slaying giants in battle, guess what? You got it—you must surround yourself with spirit-filled warriors with the hearts and weapons needed to fight the good fight of faith.

By surrounding yourself with well-equipped warriors, you set yourself up for battles that will result in countless victories. The people we surround ourselves with have the biggest influence on our behavior, our attitudes, and most importantly our *results*. The people we choose can cause us to think, say, do, and even develop into someone not aligned with who God predestined us to be.

Choose your circle wisely! Eventually, without knowing it, you will organically become your circle. Developing their habits (both good and bad), thinking like they think, and behaving like they behave. *As iron sharpens iron, so a friend sharpens a friend* (Proverbs 27:17 NLT).

When considering who to spend your time with, remember, "You are what you eat, and choosing the right circle is vital to your survival." Exercise mindfulness for who you allow to cultivate and develop the growth pattern of your circle.

The dream in your heart may be bigger than the environment you find yourself in. Sometimes, you have to move beyond your environment to see that dream fulfilled. Many people in your life are good people, but they may not be good for you. Selecting these people wisely will not only help you create a healthy circle, but will allow you to reach your goals and propel you, helping you achieve more than you can imagine. Surrounding yourself with forward thinkers will encourage you to think beyond your circumstances and take steps toward your dreams. Ephesians 3:20 says, *Now unto him that is able to do exceedingly abundantly above all that we ask or think, according to the power that worketh in us* (KJV).

This was a vital lesson I had to learn.

As a military spouse, I quickly learned the importance of a strong circle with common interests and goals. So, with each new assignment, the mission remained the same—find a group that empowered me, inspired me, and supported me. When I arrived at every new station, I was determined to find "that circle," one that would meet these needs.

MANY PEOPLE IN YOUR LIFE ARE GOOD PEOPLE, BUT THEY MAY NOT BE GOOD FOR YOU.

Finding a circle that met those requirements was never hard for me. With each set of new orders to our next location, I made friends pretty easy. It wasn't until we received orders to the Last Frontier, that this became a challenge.

Moving from Florida to Alaska was the first drastic change. We left twelve years—yes—twelve years of beautiful, sunny weather, emerald waters, and white beaches to head to the land of moose, negative temperatures, and months of darkness. As a seasoned Air Force spouse, this was not my first move. However, it was the first time in many years that we elected to live on the Air Force base.

Everything around was seemingly different. This was a training base, so the majority of the population was young airmen, officers, and their families. At this point, my husband had served 20-plus years active duty service. We lived through six deployments, six moves, and a 365-day remote tour to Korea. What did I have in common with a base full of newbies?

To my surprise, in spite of all the differences, our goals were the same. We wanted to thrive in cold weather, stay positive in the long seasons of darkness, create a closer relationship with our heavenly Father, and gain spiritual growth. These common goals led me to a community—real community. A community that forever changed my life. According to research by social psychologist Dr. David McClelland of Harvard, "[the people you habitually associate with] determine as much as 95 percent of your success or failure in life."

The blistering winters of Alaska bring frigid temperatures, and then comes darkness. According to a 1992 study published in the *American Journal of Psychiatry*, nearly 10 percent of Alaskans suffer from Seasonal Affective Disorder (SAD), a type of depression stemming from decreased daylight. Knowing this fact, I became determined to find a circle to help me to grow when the sun dimmed and disappeared.

I ventured to the Chapel in search of like-minded individuals. Conversation after conversation led me to the circle I needed. As October approached, the season of darkness fell, and coldness replaced warm sunlight. But I met the ladies who propelled me into growth.

Every Tuesday, we were committed. We gathered around the table, shared meals, scriptures, and plans for the future. We were surrounded by darkness and cold, but we reminded each other daily that we were better together. This circle was exactly what I needed to survive the lack of sunlight and to cultivate the plan God had for my life.

Thessalonians 5:11 says, *So encourage one another and build each other up, just as you are already doing* (NLT).

These ladies of faith became my spiritual lifeline. The community that was formed out of need became a necessity, and ultimately, my source of survival. Proverbs 13:20 promises, *Walk with the wise and become wise; associate with fools and get in trouble* (NLT). A strong circle makes you better and can help you weather anything.

KENNITA WILLIAMS believes that life is too short to not live life on purpose. As a Certified Life Coach and Motivational Speaker, and most importantly, Daughter of the King. Kennita's mission is to help people awaken to the possibilities in their personal and professional lives. Through spiritual principles, real life stories, provocative questions, and a fresh perspective, Kennita inspires audiences to take the first step... "One Step in the Right direction equals progress, and progress leads to purpose". Warm, genuine and engaging, Kennita's keynotes and workshops combine thought-provoking content, down to earth anecdotes, and practical strategies, leaving participants feeling uplifted and inspired. Kennita is the CEO/Founder of Model for the King Life Coaching L. L. C. Her latest project is her book, titled *Free to See* which is currently available for pre-sale. The book provides practical ideas to help people live more mindful and intentional lives. Kennita Williams is military spouse, mother of two, and a certified life coach. She has walked a path from not seeing a clear vision to knowing God's purpose for her life. Through her writing, she encourages women to be all God has planned for them to be. She serves as the Special Assistant to Senator Lisa Murkowski of Alaska. She's also a victim's advocate. She lives in North Pole, Alaska.

Chapter Sixteen
STEP FORWARD IN FAITH

SONIA GARZA

THIS IS A testimonial, a transformation story—this is my story.

The spring of 2019 hit me hard. Let me take you back to that year. Christmas in our house is always a fun time. We relish in the delights of holiday decorations, with lights and garlands galore. We loved doing "Christmas," and we were excited to build family traditions with our kids. We did it all. Cookie decorating? Check. Driving to see holiday lights? Check! This particular Christmas, however, was different than others. For this Christmas season, we were gearing up for yet another deployment, our eighth long term separation.

Being a special forces family was, and is, something I am proud to be a part of. But after almost twelve years of marriage as a military spouse, I have struggled to find my identity inside a world that revolves around the service member. I was always known as *his* wife, even when I had firmly planted my feet in my own career path.

Yet again, my husband bid us farewell, and my children hugged their daddy goodbye. We set off on a six-month journey that would forever change my life.

As with any deployment, I dove in. I plunge hard and head-first. I say "yes" to *ALL* the things: Family Readiness Group committees, Parent Teacher Association volunteering, and extra jobs here and there. I have always—and when I say always, I mean *always*—survived deployments this way. I figured that if I was busy, time would go by faster, and it does. The never ending, tick-tocking days would somehow fly by with this proven method.

But what I didn't realize was that I was fading, and fading fast. I had loaded myself with activity after activity, obligation after obligation. I was running at a pace that was completely unsustainable. But I didn't realize it. Does this sound familiar?

I had convinced myself that I was a functioning member of society, doing all the things that were asked of me, and more. I was proud of myself for holding everything together so well, smiling at everyone as they passed me by. I was my "cheery" self... still the "sunshine girl." But at night, the truth came out. I would put the kids down for the night and sit alone. That loneliness was suffocating and excruciating. I felt empty. I felt hollow. And I couldn't figure out why—until two friends came to me one night.

These two friends were my military buddies. I had done life with them—coffee meetups, after-school playdates, and birthday parties. Our friendship was rooted in deep talks about life, and family, and God. You see, what I didn't know was that God was using these women to bring me to faith—and closer to Him.

I grew up going to Catholic church on Sundays (well, most Sundays). My elementary years were brought up in a Christian school. I considered myself a Christian woman, for the most part, but I had lost my faith. The deployment was wearing me thin. My children were wearing me down. My cup was left empty.

And that's when my military spouse friends, Ana and Liza, came and saved me. They said they needed to come, and so on a dreary Washington night in March, they showed up, sat me down on my couch, and confronted me. It was an intervention. This is how the conversation went.

"I see you. I see you doing *all* the things you can. But I see you living an empty life. God loves and cares for you. He sees you and wants you to come to Him."

In that moment, I was shocked. *How had they known? How did they know my innermost thoughts? How did they see through my smiles and facade? How did they know the whispered prayers of my heart?* But they did. God did too. And in that moment, all I could do was cry.

I sobbed to be seen, to be heard. I cried to find clarity in a cloudy existence. I yearned for wisdom and strength to find my life again. My friends spread their arms and enveloped me in their love, comfort, and support. And in my stubbornness, they loved me still.

Through those beautiful friends of mine, friends who walked in Christ and came to me, I realized what I had needed all along. How brave must they have been to do that for me.

The very next day, a neighbor dropped off some items inside my home, stood at the doorway and said, "Huh, have you changed anything in here? It feels different."

I felt His nudge and knew that the "change" was God. I had finally let Him into my heart and home again, and it felt so good.

Shortly after, I started attending church with my military spouse friend, Alana. She had encouraged me to go with her for years. I had always found an excuse. But this time I went, and every sermon felt like it was just for me. I finally allowed myself to have a conversation with God. And then He tested me.

That summer, I put all of my hopes in a potential job opportunity. I thought this *job* would satisfy everything I ever wanted. It would finally give me the self-worth I had been seeking. I would get the recognition I deserved and would feel valuable, proving my six years as a military stay-at-home spouse were not in vain. I mean, I would finally have it all, right? Or so I thought.

> **THROUGH THOSE BEAUTIFUL FRIENDS OF MINE, FRIENDS WHO WALKED IN CHRIST AND CAME TO ME, I REALIZED WHAT I HAD NEEDED ALL ALONG.**

I had recommitted my life to Christ, however, a part of my heart worried that it would take me away from my family. I prayed for wisdom and discernment, and I asked what He wanted for my life. I wanted to be available to my children when my husband was away. I wanted to be the kind of mother, spouse, and friend that was present, truly present. I knew that walking away from the job was what I needed to do, and it hurt. I ached and mourned for a long while, but I ultimately knew that God was behind everything.

The year 2019 rocked me off my feet, and I found myself on my knees, surrendering to God time after time. But I was not alone.

As I walk in faith, I am finding that more military sisters-in-arms are coming forward and encouraging others to do the same. Together, we are equipping each other to live a life we desire—a life that's true to God. And it takes that village of military spouses to lead us, guide us, and show us who He is, through their love and grace.

Now, I am finding that God is at work in all things we do. He is there during our highest highs, lowest lows, and everything in between.

Here's the truth. We are all seeking something. We put our value, worth, and identity in other labels: the PTA volunteer, the working mom, the entrepreneur. But I speak from experience when I tell you those things will leave you empty unless you lead with Him. Our true identity can only be found in Christ. He was and is there for you. He is the only one that will fulfill you in ways you can't imagine.

My transformation was slow and quick, all at the same time. My hopes are that my story, in all its perfect imperfection, will inspire you to open your heart to the Lord. Surrender your hurt, your brokenness, and your fears to Him. I know you may feel unseen, isolated, and utterly alone, but it cannot be further from the truth. You are so loved. You are so special. All you need now is to say "yes." Join us on our walk with Jesus, as we step forward in faith. You belong, and you belong with us.

(See Sonia Garza's bio in Chapter Four)

Part Four

HEROES THROUGH HEARTBREAK: GRIEF, LOSS, AND POST TRAUMATIC STRESS

Chapter Seventeen
NO GREATER GIFT

CHANDEE ULCH

MOST OF MY life I lived in envy of those people who knew their God-given purpose from childhood. You know the type, the kid at age three who says she is going to be a doctor, and then does it.

For the most part, that wasn't me, except when it came to motherhood. My one God-given purpose was to be a mom. I wanted lots of children. So, when my expectation came with difficulties, I had two choices—become determined, or quit. I have never been a quitter.

Having my daughter was pure joy for me. The pregnancy was easy, no morning sickness and I didn't gain too much weight. It was afterward when all the complications occurred. The doctors messed up, making it difficult for me to have more children. Of course, I didn't learn about it until my first miscarriage.

My husband, William, and I got a second opinion. We

learned it was much worse than what we were told. Over the years, my condition resulted in a mix of twenty-three procedures, trying to repair all the damage done by my first pregnancy. Doctors shared my hope that I could have more children.

Lying in bed at night, anguishing over the thought of never feeling another life growing inside of me, prayer became my companion. My mind raced to fostering children or adoption as options. I also considered the pros and cons of continuing to put my body through the battle of another birth. There in the darkness, I made a bargain with God—if He would allow us to have another child, I would pursue all avenues until He closed every door.

To help with this endeavor financially, William decided to join the South Carolina National Guard in 2006. He assured me the guard deployed less. But the joke was on him. Within a few months of him signing the dotted line, he was headed to Iraq. Of course, days before he left, I found out we were expecting another child.

They did an ultrasound, and I got to see the baby and the heartbeat. They did my blood work, and it looked great. The doctor then came in and asked me when I wanted to schedule my abortion. I was in shock.

WHAT? How dare this man? Does he know what I have been through?

I looked at him, and as calmly as I could said, "If God wants this baby by His hands, He can have it. But it won't be by mine."

The doctor then continued to tell me why this was a selfish and inconsiderate decision for my daughter. After all, she was "going to be left an orphan, because her father was going to die in Iraq and I would die having this baby."

At twenty-four weeks, they hospitalized me. And at thirty-two weeks, they called William home from Iraq, mentally prepared to bury either his son, me, or both of us. But my doctor wasn't God.

Our now thirteen-year-old boy is taller than me. We named him Matthias Hezekiah, meaning "the gift of God that God strengthens." And he has lived up to the name.

I wish I could say this was a beautiful ending to a wonderful story. But it is not. Remember, I said I wanted lots of children. Now I don't know about you, but two children doesn't quite seem like "lots" to me. And after all I had put my body through, all kinds of heck to have more children, I figured, why stop now?

In 2009, we were active duty. The Army had us stationed in Georgia. And true to military form, William was being deployed. Shortly after William was assigned to Third Infantry Division, I learned I was pregnant again. However, this time the doctors' opinions were hopeful. Yet, all the news was not positive.

In June, William's mother informed us his only sister had been diagnosed with cancer, and it didn't look good. I could see the stress of preparing for a deployment burdening my husband. He was also worried about the pregnancy. And his sister weighed on his mind.

This pregnancy had me sicker than the others. And there was a nagging sensation in my spirit, which wouldn't let me get overjoyed. I felt guilty about it. I couldn't tell William, and I knew no one in the area I could confide in. I kept it to myself.

One night lying in bed, I felt the baby move. I woke William up, trying to get him to feel the movement as well. I thought maybe if he felt the baby, then I could relax a little. I wanted to feel excited about this life inside of me. But William felt nothing.

By the end of June, we were told if William wanted to see his sister alive, he'd better go home. We made arrangements to drive to Michigan by July. The day before we were scheduled to leave, I started feeling sick and knew I needed to go to the emergency room.

When we got there, they took me to a room. A nurse came in, and she kept repeatedly telling us we were going to see the head of the hospital. He walked in with a silent, stern military demeanor. As he examined me in silence, his cold hands felt as though they were violating me.

He finished, and with a blank look on his face, informed me my problem was nothing but an infection. He said I was overreacting. He told me I could have waited for an appointment with my regular OBGYN. I told him of our plans to head to Michigan, and he said it was fine to go.

We spent two wonderful weeks with the family in Michigan, and William was able say good-bye to his sister. As we were driving home, I began to feel sick. William pulled over to let me lie down in the back. I looked up at William and said, "Tell me the time, honey." He knew something was seriously wrong.

William called 911, asking for the location of the nearest hospital, then crossed three lanes in front of two eighteen wheelers to exit onto a small road that led to a band-aid facility. When we got into the ER, the look on the doctor's face reflected pure panic. He said, "We can't handle this at our hospital." They quickly transported me to Erlanger East Hospital.

As they wheeled me into the room, someone asked, "If you deliver tonight, your baby will be almost twenty-nine weeks old, which means there will be potential for significant complications. Do you want us to try to save the baby?"

"Do everything you can to save my baby." I said.

The doctor tried to stop my contractions.

William was standing beside me by then—never had I seen fear in his eyes before.

The doctor looked at me and said, "I need to deliver the baby, or I am going to lose you both. You have to push!"

"NO!" I knew my baby wasn't ready. I felt every kick inside of me, each kick was like a tiny heartbeat trying to fight to stay alive. *How could I push that out?*

William said, "I can't lose you. Please."

Malachi weighed only one pound and five ounces when he left my womb and entered the world, but he fought to live. The staff tried to save him, until they realized my infection had infected our son. There was nothing anyone could do. They handed Malachi to us, so we could spend as much time with him as possible before the end. Wrapped in his father's arms, Malachi took his last breath on earth, and his first breath before our Heavenly Father.

The kids were in another room, waiting on my family from North Carolina to pick them up. Before the family arrived, they had moved me into a private room. The staff asked if I wanted to have Malachi in the room with us.

"Yes, but when the kids leave," I said.

They brought Shina, our eight-year-old, and Matthias, our three-year-old, into the room. The nurse, not realizing the kids were with me, came in with the baby. She quickly tried to turn around, but Shina asked, "Mom, is that my brother?"

I knew I had to let her see him to understand what was going on. I waved the nurse over. Shina sat on the bed, with me holding Malachi. She unwrapped his blanket looking at him. "Mom, he is so cute. Can I take him home? I can put him with my dolls on my bed. I will take really good care of him, I promise."

We talked about how Malachi was in heaven with her great-grandfather. It was hard for an eight-year-old to understand, but I also knew it was something God would use to her benefit. At eighteen years old now, she understands the importance of life. She learned from her brother, Malachi, how to value it.

The next few days, I stayed in the hospital to heal. The staff kept asking if we wanted Malachi taken out of the room, but I couldn't let them remove him. He was gone, but I wasn't ready to let go. When the time came for us to leave, we found out William's unit wasn't going to come and get Malachi's body for a few days.

THE PROCESS OF HEALING REQUIRED PATIENCE, PRAYER, AND PERSEVERANCE.

I said, "You wouldn't leave a soldier behind, and we aren't leaving our son."

We pushed the elevator button and left with our white Styrofoam cooler in hand. I kept praying, *Please, don't let anyone be leaving with their baby right now. I don't think I can handle it, Lord.*

God was gracious. No one got on the elevator with a little one.

William and I strapped the cooler into our vehicle and headed to North Carolina.

As we stood at the front door of the funeral home with a white Styrofoam cooler, a gentleman answered the door. He had a kind look on his face. Taking the cooler from my husband, he disappeared. When he returned, he had only papers.

It is done, I thought. We had delivered our son to the funeral home. It seemed so wrong that his body could fit into a white Styrofoam cooler. This is how I knew for certain we live in a fallen world.

Malachi left this world in July 2009. William deployed October 2009. Our family would not be completely back together again until almost two years later in Germany. Standing in a foreign country beside my husband, I realized we were grieving for the first time together, over the loss of our son, his sister, and the after-effects of deployments and miscarriages.

The process of healing required patience, prayer, and perseverance. God showed me I needed time to allow both William and me to grieve, each in our own way. God knows exactly what every person needs. As much as God was there for me, He was there for William in a different way. Many times, as humans, we tend to see different as wrong. I am thankful God has given me eyes to see different as simply different.

I know the power of prayer. I also know, there are times when prayer feels impossible. During those times I simply say, "Jesus." It sounds simplistic, but there is power in His name. When no words come to my mind, and nothing but tears and pain surround me, I pray the name above all others, *Jesus*. I pray for my husband, children, and family.

Life is hard, plain and simple. But we can either quit or persevere. I have learned perseverance is always a much better choice. It makes us wiser, matures us, and for William and me, it has strengthened our marriage.

My God-given purpose hasn't gone the way I dreamed it would as a child. Do I have "lots" of children? Yes. They are not all with me. Some are waiting with our Lord in Heaven. Two of them, we have been blessed to raise. Through it all, God has taught me how to draw close to Him. I can imagine no greater gift than that—on earth or in heaven.

(See Chandee Ulch's bio in Chapter Nine)

Chapter Eighteen
LIFE IS WHAT HAPPENS

GRACE TUESDAY

JOHN LENNON SANG about life happening to us in his song, *Beautiful Boy*.

In Proverbs 19:21, it is written, *many are the plans in a person's heart, but it is the LORD'S purpose that prevails* (NIV).

Trusting in the journey God has planned for our purpose is easier said than done. Relinquishing control of my life to God and trusting in His plan has been a struggle. But, I am continually reminded that He is never wrong.

The script of my life certainly has not gone as I believed it would. I am happily married, but for the second time. And I do not have the tight-knit family I hoped for as a child. My life has been riddled with immeasurable grief, which has deeply impacted me. Yet, I hang on to the promise that while I am making plans, God is orchestrating a life filled with purpose for me.

For many, it is hard to comprehend that God would allow pain and suffering for any of us. But why would God allow His son's life to end in trauma and suffering, and not allow pain to be a part of ours? The fact is, God never promised us a life without hurts, but He promised He would never leave us in our most difficult times.

On more than one occasion, I have been asked how I can believe in a God who would make me a mother of three children, only to take two of them from me. I will admit to having wrestled with that same question.

The simple answer is, I believe in a God who leads me through my pain and grief, helps me stay strong, and softens my heart. Losing two of my children has deepened my faith and gifted me with a more intimate relationship with God. I have learned to lean into Him during the hardest of times. My grief has taught me deep compassion for others who are struggling. It has provided me the ability to sit with someone who is suffering unimaginable grief and offer a pillar of support. Even when our Lord felt far away, I reached for Him to guide me through the darkness.

I have endured an unbearable kind of grief that only a select group of people have felt. None of us wanted to join. Yet, I make myself a member of this club with fear of judgement.

Two of my three children have been alienated from my life for nearly nine years. Though they are not dead, I grieve the loss of them as if they are. I fear that parents who have buried a child will think I have no right to compare. My children still walk this earth. But they left my home as children and are now adults I no longer know.

No matter how a child is lost, one must endure the anguish. I have a friend whose infant child died in her arms. She compassionately told me she thinks my hell is worse than hers, because she knows her son is with God. She said when he left this earth, he knew she loved him. There is no closure to my loss.

I don't believe either of us have endured a pain greater than the other. I cannot imagine the depth of her grief. Yet, I too, have packed up two bedrooms of childhood memories, missed milestones, and experienced unfulfilled dreams.

Parental alienation takes place when one parent slowly turns a child against the other parent. It involves psychological manipulation. The estrangement may manifest itself as fear, disrespect, or hostility toward the alienated parent, as well as extending to other relatives.

> **I HAVE ENDURED AN UNBEARABLE KIND OF GRIEF THAT ONLY A SELECT GROUP OF PEOPLE HAVE FELT. NONE OF US WANTED TO JOIN.**

My two eldest children were alienated from me by their father, my ex-husband. Seven years after my sons refused to come home, I was faced with the battle of a lifetime, as my daughter also succumbed to the pressure of parental alienation. This blow was one I didn't think I could withstand. Our case was what the judge who presided called, "the worst case of alienation [he] had ever seen."

There were scores of court appearances where the events of the past were recounted. It took several years and exhausted me, to fight for my daughter's mental, physical, and emotional well-being. The physical manifestations of the stress caused me to lose hair, gain weight, have difficulty concentrating, and suffer insomnia. Getting through each day happened by the grace of God and the support of my husband, who at times had to physically hold me upright.

Coming to the realization that my children were never coming home cut me to the core. It took me two years to find the courage to begin packing their things, and another year after that to complete the process. The situation smothered me with an indescribable sense of darkness. A family member once tried to compare empty nest syndrome to how I attempted to describe my feelings. I assured her this in no way compared to the sadness that comes with that of rite of passage.

Losing a child is never normal, and it is not something just anyone can relate to, unless they have personally experienced it. This sort of finality forces one to pack away the sweet memories and abruptly ended dreams, and then put the boxes up on a shelf and attempt to move on.

God never leaves us in our times of darkness, but there are times when He feels far away. We must rely on faith alone to navigate this darkness and trust that God will lead us to the light. The waves of grief will vary from day to day. Sometimes the tide of grief will be low—the ebb and flow barely felt. Other days it will hit hard, unexpectedly, like a groundswell. Those are the days in which finding the light in the darkness seems impossible. For a long time, those days were a common occurrence for my life. Those were the days that simply getting out of bed was a win.

Re-emerging from the deep depression I felt after my children left took years. And when I did heal, I was not unscathed or without walls. I clung to my faith in God and trusted Him to lead the way. Despite my grief, there were times I laughed. But there was always a lingering distrust, waiting for the wall of darkness to come again. In time, a foreign, yet freeing feeling arrived, when I laughed and found myself realizing that the darkness didn't follow. It didn't mean I wasn't sad, but it meant I could feel joy again.

It is natural to want the pain to end, so we can feel what we call "normal." I once heard someone who had suffered the loss of a child say he wanted his head to feel right again. Another person replied, "Your child died. Your head will never feel right again."

That was a pivotal moment for me. I had to stop trying to feel the way I used to, because, no matter what, I would never feel that way again. I could never erase this loss. This realization brought to mind Luke 17:32, *Remember Lot's wife!* (NIV).

This verse is a reminder of Lot and his wife, running from Sodom and instructed not to look back. As Lot's wife ran, she yearned after her home and turned. When she did, she was immediately turned into a pillar of salt. By looking back, she was essentially, turning her back on God and failing to trust in His way. Immeasurable grief can leave us unsure that God is in control.

Learning to completely surrender to God's divine way doesn't happen overnight. Wrestling with doubt, fear, and insecurity are all part of learning to trust our Lord. Allowing ourselves to feel joy, despite incredible pain, takes time. When suffering from such an immense loss, such as that of a child, the only desire is to go back. Finding the courage to look ahead seems impossible. There are reminders everywhere, and pain physically rips through your body. But, there are things we can do to help us work our way through the sorrow.

When mourning, it is essential to be gentle with yourself. Allow yourself to feel the grief, and even the anger that comes with it. Trust that God will lead you through your pain, and He will never leave you.

Each day, week, and month, you will see new light coming through the cracks into the darkness. Soon those cracks will turn into windows, and the windows will become doors. We don't move on from such a grave loss, but we move forward in a new, changed spirit. This can provide a new perspective and lift us to a higher consciousness. When light breaks into the darkness, it brings into view God's divine plan. This is what happens when we trust.

GRACE TUESDAY is a military wife, a Health and Nutrition Educator, a speaker, and a published author. She strives to empower others to discover their truest self and to go beyond being defined by one's circumstances through developing deep trust and hope in God. She promotes self-care through proper nutrition as an important part of healing. Grace works to advocate for legislation that will provide better shared-parenting laws and restore relationships of alienated parents and children. Grace's story, *God's Perfect Timing*, is published in *Blessings in Disguise*, an anthology of Christian stories, and has been a contributing author to Milspo Co. When she is not working, you can find Grace running, hiking, or spending time with her husband and their Bassett Hound. Connect with Grace and follow her blog, *Our Daily Tuesday* at www.gracetuesday.com.

Chapter Nineteen
HOW TO "LEAN IN" TO THE PAIN OF OTHERS

JOLYNN LEE

UNFORTUNATELY, DEATH IS not an uncommon event in our experience. After being married to the military for thirty years, I know how much this unspoken sentence hovers over every exercise, deployment, and event our spouses engage in. Our children are aware of the reality. We discuss the "business of 'what if'" frequently, as we ensure paperwork is in order and the plan of operation for "in the event of" is clearly laid out and established.

We have encountered loss multiple times throughout our stint in military life, for a variety of reasons. But it wasn't until recently, I became the initial phone call in someone else's trauma and heartbreak.

One the volunteers with REBOOT Combat Recovery,

Camp Lejeune, passed away, and his wife chose to call my phone number first. It was my first exposure as the initial phone call, that first conversation following a death. In our previous military experience, there was always a chaplain or Casualty Assistance Calls Officer (CACO) who contacted the family and weathered those fresh, raw emotions.

My phone rang at 4:06 a.m. and my brain raced thinking: *Who on earth is calling me this early on a Saturday?*

I was shocked into awareness when I heard the hysteria on the other end of the line, and I frantically tried to place the voice. It was gut-wrenching, as I ran through a mental rolodex of voice recognition, trying to identify the crying woman on the phone. When she finally announced herself and started explaining what happened, I was stunned into speechlessness. Literally, our friend and avid volunteer had spoken at our graduation just five days prior. As it happens so frequently with loss, this tragedy was totally unexpected.

That call made me deeply appreciative of some lessons I learned in our military career, one of which is the encouragement to just be present in the midst of sorrow. When we step into the grief of another person, there are no magic words or techniques that will immediately lift their pain and transform their circumstance. But, it is vitally important to be fully with them in the midst of their situation. Too often, individuals want to turn away, because they fear saying the wrong thing or making matters worse. At a time when the hurting need to be surrounded the most—they are often abandoned out of fear.

Grief, especially in our military community, tends to drive people away—maybe because when death occurs, it is a very real reminder that it can happen to anyone. And we like to pretend that what our loved ones do is honorable, but safe.

I will never forget a conversation we shared with our dear

friends at their kitchen counter. The husband, an active duty spouse, was sharing his "near miss experiences" with us, when his wife, who was quietly doing the dishes, spoke up and said, "Why have you never shared this with me before?"

His reply was simple, "You don't want to know about the near misses—you just want to know that I am good."

Understandable. When death occurs, it brings reality home. For some people, that reality spotlights the potential for tragedy, and they would rather turn away than lean into the grief of others. When I answered that early morning phone call, I mentally checked my own emotions, so I could be present in the midst of the situation. I needed to attune to the feelings of the spouse who was grieving, to be supportive, and to provide guidance in the midst of her devastating loss.

Once her hysteria calmed, we worked through some of the practical facts. I asked if paramedics had been called and where she was physically located. Her husband had passed from a sudden stroke in his sleep. He woke her with an inability to breathe that rapidly progressed without warning. Even as she shared the story with me, she shifted her focus. "At least he didn't suffer. He didn't seem to be in pain. He just left me, quickly."

As we continued to talk, she immediately turned to his involvement with our organization as a volunteer and the joy it brought him in recent years, thus explaining her call to me. Our group had brought him peace as he recovered from his own combat trauma, and she was hoping we could do the same for her. I offered her the assurance that we would walk alongside her and assist her as she navigated both the Veteran's Administration process, and the emotional and spiritual transition of loss.

I gently reminded her where her husband was now, as he was a strong believer in the Lord, and she took comfort in that fact. After we had spoken for an extended period of time, I offered to come and join her at her location. She assured me she was calmer and said she didn't need me to be physically present at that moment. But she did ask if she could please call again. We set a time and location to meet, so she would have the tangible assurance she was not alone.

Throughout that first day, I checked in on her. "Do you have food? Are you secure physically? Do you have access to finances? Are you alone?"

But her main focus was on notifying friends and family. She even requested that I contact some people on her behalf.

A few days later, when we again sat down in person, I learned that her husband had been the lead on most decisions and all finances, so we established a trusted point of contact from whom she could seek guidance (her father).

One of the key points Dr. H. Norman Wright makes in his book, *The Complete Guide to Crisis and Trauma Counseling*, is when dealing with loss is that, "It is important to show continual support and concern for the bereaved in tangible ways for two to three months after the death—sending cards, making phone calls or taking an occasional meal" (p. 245). This guidance encouraged me to establish a meal train for future weeks, to support this woman once the initial shock passed.

It is easy for outside individuals to move on following a death, but for those on the inner circle, the process is much more layered. The support for those going through the process of loss and grief needs to be long-term, not temporary.

We have since invited this widow to organizational events, so she would know her place is with us, even in the absence of her husband. But we did so with the reminder to participate at her personal comfort level. Dr. Wright states that those who are grieving need safe spaces, safe people, and safe situations in which to heal. It should be the goal of those closest to the individual dealing with grief and loss, to provide them with the establishment of safe space to facilitate healing long-term—without judgement, pressure, or time constraints.[1]

Grief is messy. It doesn't look the same in every person. Mourning and loss are very personal and individual journeys. For those near the ones who experience loss, it is our privilege to support them. However, we may need to encourage them in a language they can receive. It is not our place to judge the decisions they may make as they navigate very broken roads. Instead, we should speak wisdom with compassion in support of the decisions they make, as they rebuild their lives and establish a new normal.

> **THE SUPPORT FOR THOSE GOING THROUGH THE PROCESS OF LOSS AND GRIEF NEEDS TO BE LONG-TERM, NOT TEMPORARY.**

There are no words that can soothe the brokenness of the soul when loss is experienced, but the presence of companionship can bind up hurt and restore hope. I strongly encourage others to "lean in" to the messiness of grief. Do not let those suffering do so alone. It is easy to assume they have support from friends and family. But, so often when grief comes—those primarily affected spend much of their time and energy comforting others, rather than receiving comfort. Provide that safe space for them to land, that soft haven of companionship, distant enough from the direct woundedness, so they can unburden themselves freely and without guilt. Allow them to experience their own pain, secure in the knowledge they don't have to do so alone.

Walk beside them, not just through the initial days, but in

---

[1] Wright, N. (2011). *The complete guide to crisis & trauma counseling: what to do and say when it matters most!* Ventura, CA: Regal Publishing.

the weeks and months to come. And then step forward to cheer for them, as they start to rebuild life and live again. You will never regret holding the hand of someone else in their time of need. Pouring out from your own well into another individual who is broken and dry, will fill your cup. You may not do it flawlessly—none of us are perfect—but it is the willingness to do it in our own blemished way that matters most.

(See Jolynn Lee's bio in Chapter Ten)

Chapter Twenty
THE JOURNEY THROUGH LOSS, INFERTILITY, AND GOD'S MIRACLES

WENDI IACOBELLO

D**ID YOU KNOW** that 37.3% of active duty married military couples have children, compared to 13.9% who are married without children? Well, my spouse and I have been a part of that 13.9% statistic for quite a while.[2]

You may wonder if the vast majority of couples with children increased pressure on us to start a family. In some ways, yes, they did. We felt very much like outsiders in a world saturated with children. Your classification as a "family" relied heavily on

---

[2] Source: 2018 Demographics Profile of the Military Community (Department of Defense) https://www.militaryonesource.mil/reports-and-surveys/infographics/active-duty-member-and-family-demographics

whether you had children or not. We also married later in life. I was 36, and my hubby-to-be was 29 on our wedding day. Being older when we married made the urge to have kids greater, too.

After a year of trying to have a baby, we had a positive pregnancy test. It was such a magical moment. I'll never forget how filled with joy my husband was when I reported the news with him. We phoned our closest family and friends to share our excitement. We also set up our very first obstetrical exam with my longtime doctor an hour away. The office was a far drive from my military station with my husband, but only ten minutes from my job of nine years.

Then, my husband left for three weeks of training in another state. Meanwhile, my mother stepped up and accompanied me to the doctor. I was filled with excitement and nerves, because I did not know what to expect.

After sitting through an hour of information exchange with the nurse about how to take care of myself and the baby, it was time to see this little nugget on the ultrasound.

I was around eight weeks, so the ultrasound was performed trans-vaginally. We facetimed my husband during this moment, and suddenly, we saw our little baby on the screen. We both smiled, while the ultrasound tech looked puzzled. She politely explained that she would be right back, and in that moment, my heart began to race.

She returned with a doctor, who also scanned my insides using the ultrasound wand. The physician peered at the images of our baby, and then at me, with a serious look on her face. She told me the words no pregnant woman wants to hear, "There is no heartbeat."

At that moment, the world stopped spinning, and my heart shattered into a million pieces. As serious talks began about how to remove the baby, I froze in pain. I could not even speak. I could see lips moving, but I was paralyzed in time and could not hear anything.

When the scheduled day to remove my baby from my body arrived, my husband and I prayed over him and said an emotional goodbye prior to entering the doctor's office. We elected to have genetic testing done on our child's remains to get answers.

Weeks later, we found out the sex of our baby, and that he had a genetic disorder, which is why his tiny heart stopped beating. Learning this threw me into another wave of pain and sorrow. I wondered how much suffering he had to endure, due to his condition, during his short time in my womb.

Being a childless couple was extremely isolating for us, especially after we experienced pregnancy loss. It was as if we had a disease, and people did not want to get "infected." We were in extreme despair, without much support. People also offered comforting words online that were far from comforting. Friends with children pushed us away, causing me to become very bitter, as I felt my worth as an individual was highly centered on whether or not I could produce a child. I continued to fall into a deep, dark hole.

Then, just when I thought my life couldn't be more tragic, I lost my thirteen-year-old beagle, who was my best friend prior to military life. I became stricken with fear of what or who I might lose next. I also blamed God for all of this sadness and grief. *Why me? What have I done to deserve so much loss at once?* I just couldn't understand, and I wanted to hide away forever.

Three months after losing my dog, I walked away from my nine-year career in higher education. I just couldn't teach anymore. Remaining in the spotlight, when I wanted to cry nonstop, was not an option. Every day, I struggled to go on.

Losing a baby makes you question everything, including your faith. I questioned it so much that I turned my back on conversations with God. I couldn't understand why something so terrible had to happen to my family. Not that I wished it on anyone else, but I just couldn't fathom why we had to go through so much pain.

Family and friends tried to breathe scripture and faith back into me, but I wasn't open to it. I nodded my head, and I let it go in one ear and out the other. I kept moving without thinking about God's ways too much anymore. My soul was absolutely lost, and the enemy kept whispering terrible lies into my ear that I ended up believing for a while.

A year after losing our baby, my neighbor invited me to a women's conference at her church. After reviewing the information, I decided to sign up and give it a try. Little did I know the impact this one event would have on my life.

The first night of the conference was long, but the music and energy was amazing. The next day, I walked into the church alone. I felt a lump in my throat. When I entered the sanctuary, the music poured into my soul so hard I had to stand in the very back against the wall. After a few moments, I went to the bathroom to get tissue. The music was playing loudly through speakers. I stood there and sobbed.

For an entire year, I had been carrying this grief all by myself. I had refused to give it to God, and the load was very heavy on my soul. It was in that moment I heard God whisper, "Come back to me."

I reentered the sanctuary, and I continued to sob against the wall in the back. God once again whispered to my soul: "I never left you. I have been here the entire time waiting for you."

In that instant, I came back to faith and turned over the grief once and for all to God. I released the pain to Him and pleaded and begged His forgiveness for ever doubting his goodness.

Just then, a sweet woman near my age came back to hug and

talk with me. She prayed over my situation of loss and desire. She even explained that she had been through the same thing. This was the day my broken soul began to truly start healing.

On this path of restoration, I found my faith again. God also revealed a way for me to use the pain I endured to help others—through a mini-ministry for military couples on an infertility and loss journey. I began to talk and strategize with others about the vision God had given to me, and how it might work.

> **GOD ONCE AGAIN WHISPERED TO MY SOUL: "I NEVER LEFT YOU. I HAVE BEEN HERE THE ENTIRE TIME WAITING FOR YOU."**

I finally understood that this was my son's purpose. This ministry to help others who have also lost faith would be in his name. It gave me comfort knowing how I could turn my tragedy into triumph and do it in my son's memory. Even though his life was never lived beyond the womb, he still had a purpose.

That is the goodness of God. In our deepest, darkest moments, in our biggest struggles, when you are "in the wait," He is always there. He never leaves your side. God didn't promise us a life without trouble, but what He will do is make something beautiful rise from those painful ashes. He will create a purpose from your pain, if you just surrender and believe.

More time passed, and we were still struggling to conceive. We tried tons of holistic measures, such as acupuncture, healthy eating, adequate exercise, ovulation calendars, and more. What we didn't try yet was giving it to God. So, we did. And we finally found a peace about our situation.

While at an annual faith-based Christmas event for military families, I found myself a little somber during yet another holiday season without a child of our own. That time of year is especially hard for loss families and those struggling to bear children. In fact, we hadn't had a positive pregnancy test in twenty-one months. While watching all of the little children at this event, I began to wonder what the path to parenthood might look like for my husband and me. We had finally accepted the fact that we may not be able to have children of our own, and we were going to start the foster parent process in the New Year.

After the event, I stayed behind to speak with the pastor. While fighting back the pools filling my eyes, I explained that my husband and I had been trying for a baby for almost three years. I told him we had lost a baby, too.

My tears streamed down my cheeks, as the pastor grabbed my hand and said, "Let's pray." He called out to God over the situation, and he invited me to meet with the team of elders of his church to pray even more.

A few weeks passed, and the pastor emailed me about praying with the elders. A few days earlier, my husband and I had found out we were pregnant! When I responded to the pastor, I asked if he and the elders could please pray over my pregnancy and this miraculous baby we had been blessed with.

While I was deemed a high risk and geriatric pregnancy, due to the history of loss and my age, nine months later, I birthed a beautiful and healthy boy.

From my experience with loss, grief, and infertility, I continue to advocate for military couples without children. Through my writing and efforts behind the scenes, I run a support ministry for them. Because I have lived the heartache, I know how difficult and isolating it can be.

It is my mission and goal to ensure that military couples without children are counted as a family, and feel included among the community. It is important that childless couples feel that their worth as a family unit holds the same merit as those with children. They are part of God's miraculous family, and we should welcome them in ours. Let's be present for one another, always encouraging each other to fix our eyes on Jesus—the author and perfecter of our faith.

WENDI IACOBELLO is a graduate of Appalachian State University with a Master of Arts in Educational Media. She also has a BS degree in Early Childhood Education. Her professional career in education spans across nine years in the public education sector to include; middle and high school special education, adult education for incarcerated men, women, & youth, compensatory education, High School Equivalency instruction formerly known as GED, and community college instruction in Early Childhood Education curriculum courses. Wendi has been an Army Spouse since 2015 and became a first time mom in the fall of 2019. In addition to being a stay-at-home mom, she is a freelance writer and online education consultant. She has been published in multiple military affiliated websites and magazines such as; Fort Bragg's In-Motion Magazine, Military Spouse Magazine, and Legacy Magazine to name a few. She believes that inner strength is developed through four pillars; fitness, faith, volunteerism, and finding purpose. Her blog, Strength 4 Spouses, inspires and empowers military spouses to find and develop their inner strength to build the resiliency needed for military life. Learn more at https://strength4spouses.blog, and connect with Wendi at facebook.com/strength4spouses, www.instagram.com/strength-4spouses, & www.twitter.com/strength4s

Chapter Twenty-One
LOVING, LEAVING, AND LEARNING

BECKY HOY

IT WAS 2:00 p.m. on a Thursday. I sat in the dimly lit bathroom of a rental home we had moved into eight months earlier, fully submerging myself every few minutes to momentarily drown the sounds of my own tears.

A hot bath has always been my preferred retreat. It's my place to quite literally soak away the stress of the day. I let myself fall fully into the moment, weights lifting as the warmth and the wet divert my full focus away from concerns too heavy to carry without respite.

But this time, the weights weren't lifting. I tried desperately to concentrate on the sound of the water moving, the ripples appearing with each inhale—anything to distract from the news my husband had just shared with me. But the tears refused to listen, instead dripping and then streaming down my face. My tears turned to sobs, sobs turning to choked cries, until I again sank beneath the rapidly chilling water, hoping each time I emerged, I would open my eyes to a new reality—a life of stability and security.

As the water turned too cold to bear, I heard my more logical inner critic begin to call me out: *Becky. You. Are being. Absolutely. Ridiculous. This reaction is outrageous. Nobody has died. Nobody is sick. Nothing has been lost. You are ONLY moving to a new duty station.*

At the thought of moving, the tears began again, until I found myself under the now ice-cold water once more. And despite my best wishing, I knew the reality of our situation. Being married to an active-duty soldier does not mean stability, it does not mean security—it means swift change and little autonomy.

BEING MARRIED TO AN ACTIVE-DUTY SOLDIER DOES NOT MEAN STABILITY, IT DOES NOT MEAN SECURITY— IT MEANS SWIFT CHANGE AND LITTLE AUTONOMY.

Five years earlier, and just three months after being married, I had packed my existence into tiny boxes, leaving behind all but one person I knew and loved. This time, the Army landed my husband and me in Fort Bragg, North Carolina. We busily began the task of building a life together out of thin air. Knowing not a soul (or even a grocery store), we started the painstaking process of learning each new road, new place, and new person in our brand new "hometown."

We would end up having a storybook PCS. Within weeks, we were surrounded by friends and connected with a community of faith that would carry us through the 12-month deployment our young family was thrown into before the first change of seasons. But we knew none of this when we arrived.

We fell in love with Fort Bragg. We fell in love with the tangy taste of barbecue, the beautiful site of blooming dogwood trees, and even the sticky summers. More than anything, we fell in love with our people.

Crossroads Church had taken us in and became our home. I had grown up in the church, but this was our first chance to decide how we would live out our faith as a married couple. The people of Crossroads gave us the love we needed to navigate that new season.

Fort Bragg and the community we found there allowed us to thrive, even through nearly five years of seemingly endless separations for deployments and trainings. We grew in our marriage and our faith. Later, when I heard the Lord not-so-quietly calling me to vocational ministry, I nervously resigned from my other job to accept a position working full-time with Crossroads.

Just a few years earlier, the military had pulled us into a new life of uncertainty, in a new place with new people. Now, we found our family flourishing. We had gone from complete insecurity to overwhelming fulfillment in our marriage, our spiritual lives, and now in my own calling.

Each week as we studied together, served together, and worshipped together, the people of Crossroads Church became our closest friends. They became the people who encouraged us, challenged us, and supported us. Year after year, we celebrated holidays, welcomed little ones to the world, laughed together, cried together, and grieved together, until this circle of friends became family. And that family became the greatest gift we never would have known to ask for.

Until the news that we knew would come finally did.

My husband received orders to a new base. We were moving. We were leaving the community we loved for a new place, with new people, far from the family that had been forged over these years—far from my encouragers, challengers, and supporters. I would be starting over—again. And though I knew these relationships could never be lost, I desperately feared the reality of once again building a community from nothing.

So, I cried in the bathtub at 2:00 p.m.

I cried until my inner critic admonished me, and then I cried some more for good measure, giving into the fear we would never again find this type of love and acceptance.

It was only when I began to pray, the crying stopped. It didn't stop because I was no longer tearful—but because I was drawn to a verse so intensely, I had to give it my full attention.

"Have I not commanded you? Be strong and courageous. Do not be afraid; do not be discouraged, for the Lord your God will be with you wherever you go" (Joshua 1:9, NIV).

I remember vividly thinking, *Really, Lord? Wherever?*

Overwhelmingly I knew the answer was, *Yes. Even there.*

In the midst of my tears, I was given the verse the Lord intended to carry me through, and I clung to it, hard. I realized I did not need to fear whether I could again build a community that would embrace our family, because I had not built a community where we were. God had created it, and He invited us to be a part of it. He had done it before, and He would do it again in our new home. I did not need to fear, because it was not up to me.

As I sit here writing this, I'm looking over my calendar and I realize we are only months away from another move to accommodate my husband's military orders. I know when the news we know will come finally does, it will once again be heartbreaking. I will cry, perhaps inconsolably in my bathtub. But my tears will be different.

This time, my tears will not be for fear. I will not worry about whether we will find our people. This time, my tears will simply mourn the distance between our next home and the family that God provided us with here—in what was once a new place.

The moves of military life can seem like an impossible burden to bear. But I'm reminded as we stare forward toward the next transition, what a blessing it has been to see firsthand God's provision. The Lord does go wherever we go. We move, but He remains unmoving, and so are His promises.

(See Becky Hoy's bio in Chapter One)

Chapter Twenty-Two
A SORROW SHARED IS BUT HALF A TROUBLE

JOLYNN LEE

MY GRANNY IS gone now, but the lessons I learned from her linger on today. One of those lessons comes from a cross-stitch that hung in her hallway which read, *A sorrow shared is but half a trouble, a joy that is shared is a joy made double*. That simple mantra has carried my family through some dark times.

When trauma hit our home, it hit with a double punch. My husband came home from a deployment very changed. After an overseas tour, he suffered with insomnia, was hypersensitive to sound, and startled easily. P.T.S.D. a/k/a Post-Traumatic Stress Disorder was now a part of our daily lives.

Shortly after that, a young woman very close to us experienced a sexual assault. Suddenly, we went from the "All-

American family" to a unit of walking wounded with an internal implosion impulse no one could see. With a serious case of combat trauma, as well as PTSD because of the traumatic sexual assault of someone we cared deeply about, our family became a statistic.

All through history, there are epic tales of combat warriors who returned home broken and shattered from their experiences. One of the earliest encounters is the tale of an Athenian warrior who was literally struck blind in combat when a fellow warrior died next to him on the battlefield. The age-old term "shell shock" dates back to those returning from World War I. "Battle fatigue," "combat exhaustion," and "war stress" were used to describe veterans returning from World War II.

Meriam Webster offers a definition of trauma as "being an experience that produces psychological injury or pain." In the minds of most individuals, PTSD is considered a combat issue. However, trauma comes in many forms: a car accident, an exposure to physical violence or abuse, a natural disaster, witnessing violence, being exposed to a life-threatening experience, a major health crisis, domestic violence, childhood abuse, or sexual assault, just to name a few. Trauma hurts can leave very lasting scars on lives touched by the unexpected and unthinkable. Often, those scars are invisible, and the wounds of individuals touched by trauma are unseen.

That was us—our family had unwillingly joined the ranks of those thousands of individuals who walk among us every single day, pain unnoticed, yet they carry the scars of unmentioned battles. Often, those with PTSD are called the "walking wounded" because they walk among society with the outward appearance of normalcy, while being shattered and broken inside, hiding their dysfunction as a means of survival. They can appear as your neighbor who is always willing to lend a helping hand, or the one who seems unapproachable and grumpy, your favorite teacher, the local youth coach, your pastor, your co-worker, or even a family member you never knew experienced a trauma. Their hurts are hidden, because they still haven't found the words to express their grief. The wounds of trauma are often unrecognized or unacknowledged, until life is visibly out of control.

For the individual with PTSD, there tends to be a before and after moment, when life became impacted by trauma exposure and their worldview was markedly changed. When my husband came home, I thought I was prepared. I had been to the reintegration brief, where a summary of "what to look for in your returning combat spouse" had been presented by the Family Readiness Officer (FRO) via a PowerPoint presentation. The speaker had as much enthusiasm as an individual reading a stock report.

TRAUMA HURTS CAN LEAVE VERY LASTING SCARS ON LIVES TOUCHED BY THE UNEXPECTED AND UNTHINKABLE.

We were the good little military family, all red, white and blue. "Go America, Go Marine Corps." Little did I know how much life had changed in those months apart. Yes, I knew my husband had been shot. He earned a Purple Heart and Silver Star during that deployment. But every decoration earned comes at a cost.

That reintegration brief never told me that kids screaming and running through the house might trigger my husband and incite enormous anger responses. Hypervigilance is not easily shut down. The need to control and micromanage everything and everyone is born from an inner anxiety to keep everyone safe and to control your environment to ensure safety. The phrase "complacency kills" could very nearly kill a marriage relationship and family unity. Suddenly, my husband's inability to sleep, his dislike of people and crowds, and his desire to avoid random loud noises was overtaking our lives.

The FRO had told us to watch out for excessive drinking. But no one mentioned random binge drinking justified because it's the Marine Corps Ball, or another celebratory situation where drinking is normalized. I stayed lost in this no-man's land of only "knowing what I know" until the young woman we loved was harmed. Then it all exploded with a violence and force that the memory of, to this day, can still take my breath away.

We have our own before trauma and after trauma, marking that dark moment. The compounded trauma in our family that came with the added layer of sexual assault, changed everything.

When our second traumatic encounter happened, my husband and I were on the brink of divorce. We lived as though tiptoeing around mortar shells, never knowing what might set off emotional fireworks, or where the next negative response might come from. Conversations were almost non-existent in our home, because the continual corrective nature my husband unintentionally operated under brought a blanket of silence to almost every interaction. Mealtimes were something we endured, as my husband's attention to detail, that served him so well at work, focused in on the children's table manners or how loud we were chewing.

My husband couldn't see the need for help when it was just him hurting. But trauma doesn't happen in a bubble. Hurt people, hurt other people—my husband just didn't realize it yet. However, that reality was quickly driven home when a young lady was broken—breaking him.

What we cannot do for ourselves, we so very often will do

for the love of another. My husband needed to be healthy and strong to help someone whose life mattered very much to him. In spite of his pain, he succeeded at work. He climbed the promotion ladder and continued to perform with excellence—everywhere but at home.

But with a personal trauma hitting so close to home, suddenly home was quite obviously on fire, and it could no longer be ignored. My husband entered individual counseling. We began marriage therapy. Our family went into counseling and received therapy.

I went back to school to get a degree in counseling, because I needed to know all the details about trauma and PTSD. I desperately needed to know how to best help my family heal—mind, body and spirit. Together, we dug in our heels and sought healthy, as individuals and as a family unit. Finding help and healing became what we lived, breathed and ate. It was a mindset we had to intentionally choose from moment to moment, day to day.

I would love to tell you we were transformed overnight, but anything of value takes hard work, intentional effort, and time—and that includes the restoration of a soul. Fighting for our family, for us to find healthy after experiencing such brokenness, was the most painstakingly difficult task I have ever encountered. There were days when it seemed absolutely pointless, where we would take steps forward, just to fall back as the compounded wounds were meticulously peeled away, like the fine layers of an onion skin.

But the Bible encouraged me. *My heart overflows with a good theme...* (Psalms 45:1), reminds us to hope in the darkness. There is healing from hurt, and restoration can become a reality.

I told myself time and again: *Just keep swimming, just keep swimming.* All the while, I wondered if anyone at the school where I was teaching had a clue about what was going on in our lives. I felt alone and isolated, even when I stood in a crowd. I cried my way through the worship service at church, forcing myself to offer a sacrifice of praise out of sheer obedience. Yet, I felt furious at God for not protecting us from harm.

Guess what? That was all okay—it was all totally normal. It is 100% permissible to feel angry and tragic, to feel cheated by life or devastated by events. However, it is not okay to stay that way forever. Seasons change, and we are called to walk through the valley of trauma, not to pitch our tent and make camp in heartache forever. Trauma should be a comma in the story of your life, not the period that ends it.

Today, those things that triggered both my husband and the young woman we care for, are things of the past. The trauma our family encountered does not define us, but the healing journey has definitely become our testimony. Each member of our family has had the opportunity to use our experiences to speak into the lives of others. We are privileged to encourage people to seek help and healing. In some ways, it is like we have a radar that identifies inner brokenness in others.

We have walked a journey of healing as a result of traumatic experiences I would never wish on another. But I know there are many out there experiencing devastation every single day. And so, we speak out, we share our story because my granny's words are right, "A sorrow shared is but half a trouble—a joy that is shared is a joy made double."

When we share our sorrow and hurt, when we speak about our traumatic experience, the powerful hold that experience has on our life and spirit is diminished. Truth sets us free, and when we tell people about our healing, the joy is multiplied in the hope it gives others. The wounded dare to believe they too may find light at the end of a personal journey of darkness.

Living with hidden trauma often results in a lifestyle that is both mentally and emotionally exhausting, as the wounded attempt to mask their inner pain. However, living with trauma can also evolve into a healthy and victorious lifestyle, when you partner with others who offer support and encouragement.

If you or someone you love has experienced trauma, you are not alone. Hold onto hope—this season will pass. Restoration is possible both individually and relationally, and joy can be found in living. If we reach just one person with our example of transformation through trauma, our biography becomes our testimony. The ripple effect spreads. While it is true hurt people hurt other people, it is also true that healed people, heal other people! We don't have to save the world, God provides the encounters, we simply have to #justreachone with our story of hope.

(See Jolynn Lee's bio in Chapter Ten)

Chapter Twenty-Three
DIGGING FOR TREASURE

GRACE TUESDAY

A **STIGMA OF SHAME** often accompanies Post Traumatic Stress Disorder (PTSD). Even with mental health awareness becoming more prevalent, admitting you have a problem is still difficult for the sufferer. Service members fear that if they seek medical attention, they will be singled out, and their careers jeopardized.

My husband, a kind, compassionate man, doesn't have violent outbursts. He doesn't use any drugs and rarely consumes alcohol. Level-headed with a very good job, he doesn't suffer from depression. On the other hand, he struggles with organization, procrastinates, forgets things, and hoards items like receipts or old things he doesn't need anymore. He has a very hard time feeling deeply or being in tune with his own feelings. And he struggles to focus for a long period of time. PTSD comes in many forms, and these are the ways it has manifested in my husband.

One event can change someone forever. I don't know the man my husband was before PTSD. When I fell in love with him, he was already reeling from what he saw in Afghanistan. I could tell from the minute I met him that he was everything I had been dreaming of. But as time went on, I could also sense he was hurting, and there was something deep inside of him I couldn't reach. Much like scratching the surface of a deeply buried treasure, I found myself attempting to dig deeper into his soul to uncover what lies beneath.

One summer evening before we were married, my husband and I were enjoying dinner on the patio of a favorite restaurant. I was feeling drained that evening by things that had happened with my children earlier in the day. But I began to feel relaxed the more we talked. The stress of the day diminished, and my husband had my full attention. He began to share a story about one of his deployments to Afghanistan.

In the year we had been dating, he had shared very little about his deployments with me, and his sudden openness, while welcome, made me unsure of how to react. Vocalizing the memories brought my normally stoic husband to tears. I wasn't prepared for the details he gave or his reaction to them, and I have since wished I could go back and react differently. I know now that the shock of his tears caused me to recoil and give a much more subdued response than I would normally provide.

When my husband and I met, he had been home from his second deployment for three years. He thought the passing of time had dulled the emotional effects of what happened to him in Afghanistan. In fact, he thought it wasn't bothering him at all. At least until the evening we went to dinner, where he decided to share his experiences with me. While he was at work that day, a few comrades he had been deployed with mentioned they had been seeing therapists to learn how to cope with their PTSD.

Hearing his friends admit they were struggling and seeking help caused my husband to wonder if he had truly gotten past what he had experienced. He wondered if he would benefit from some psychotherapy as well.

After sharing his experiences that evening, we agreed that reaching out to the Veterans Administration might be beneficial. He contacted the VA the next day, and he was scheduled to see a therapist. After the initial appointment, he brought home CDs of guided meditation. Listening to these CDs was meant to help him relax and focus on something positive. We climbed into bed that evening and played one of the guided meditations. Within a few minutes, my husband grew agitated, and he quickly shut it off and went to sleep.

> **I WASN'T PREPARED FOR THE DETAILS HE GAVE OR HIS REACTION TO THEM, AND I HAVE SINCE WISHED I COULD GO BACK AND REACT DIFFERENTLY.**

The next morning, he told me he felt there was no way guided meditation would be of use to him. That was the end of that.

It is natural to want a quick fix for something that will likely take a lot of work. Unfortunately, my husband never sought further help. He has tucked away, in the back of his mind, any memory of the terrifying things he experienced during his deployments.

The man I fell in love with is the same man who, three years prior, was relaxing with his team at their Forward Operating Base in Afghanistan after a daily mission. An urgent call came in for all available soldiers to report to a nearby weapons range where a blast had occurred.

He is the same man who, upon arriving at the blast location, immediately noticed three charred, dead men on stretchers. One man was burned so badly that his arms stuck straight up into the air, the way they had been when he was struck. Another man lay in pieces, his head placed on a stretcher between his dismembered legs. My husband is the same man who sprang into action to aid a screaming man who had been hit in the head by the blast.

The man I fell in love with returned home from Afghanistan and wrestled with the memory of lifting the leg of the man with the head wound. My husband felt his leg fall into pieces, weakly held together by his skin, much like a Jacob's Ladder toy. He worried that he didn't splint the leg properly. He wondered if maybe the way he bandaged the leg wasn't tight enough to prevent the man from bleeding to death, even though he did everything within his power to save him. The man I fell in love with can still recall the smell of burning flesh that permeated the air that afternoon, and the feeling in his hands of the man's blown-apart head as he helped to move him to a stretcher.

The man that I fell in love with had, on another day of the same deployment, been driving a Ford Explorer sandwiched between two upper-armored Humvees, as he and his team were out for a mission. Without warning, he witnessed an Improvised Explosive Device (IED) detonate just feet from him, ripping off the hood of the Humvee in front of him, injuring the passengers. He jumped out of his vehicle, gun raised, ready to kill anyone who would put him or his teammates in further danger.

These are the events that my husband had to learn to push to the back of his mind. He could not allow himself to feel fear and keep focused on each assigned mission. Upon returning home, he reintegrated, to the best of his ability, into life as normal. But he is still plagued by triggers when we watch certain movies and documentaries, or by everyday things that someone else might take for granted.

Not knowing my husband prior to his deployments might be a blessing, because I have nothing to compare him to. But I feel a piece of my husband didn't come home from Afghanistan, and for that I am resentful. Resentful, not of my husband, but resentful of what is lost to me and others. I know my husband to be a strong, hard-working, God-fearing, and compassionate man. I assume he was all of these things before he deployed, but I also know that events change people. There are things I know I have missed out on experiencing because of PTSD.

My husband's struggle to stay on task, and his ability to numb his feelings, are a result of tucking his past experiences safely into the back of his mind. I often resent the way he doesn't feel emotion over a song or something sentimental that might bring others to tears. I wish he could stay focused on things a little longer, before he retreats to a far-off place in his mind. And I wish he could tell me how he feels.

Being a spouse of a service member who suffers from PTSD can feel lonely and frustrating, but it can also be filled with love, patience, and an infinite amount of pride. I know not everyone's story is the same. Some have deeper challenges, depending on the degree of PTSD haunting their homes. But regardless of where we are, we can all focus on intentional healing.

Military spouses don't invite PTSD into their marriages, whether it was present before or after the union took place. We continually fight this exhausting battle because we love a warrior. We reconcile the pieces of our lives, we put them together to create a new life, and we never stop digging for the treasure of our warrior's heart. It's there, even if it's gotten buried under a pile of post-traumatic pain.

(See Grace Tuesday's bio in Chapter Eighteen)

Part Five

TIME TO SPEAK UP: MILITARY MISSION WORK AND ADVOCACY

Chapter Twenty-Four
A MISSION OF KINDNESS

JESSICA MANFRE

I BELIEVE WE ALL have a mission in life—a mission God gently pushes us toward and equips us for. Another way to describe it is like receiving a call from Him, one where He asks us to dive into a passionate purpose that lights the soul on fire.

This may sound dramatic, but I firmly believe it to be true. The question is: do we listen to those signs from Him, or ignore them altogether?

Sometimes, I think we allow that ugly voice of self-doubt to prevent us from answering those nudges from God. Denying His call comes from a fear of the unknown or failure, speaking to our minds. *Don't listen to it!*

You can and will make a difference in the world if you believe with all your heart and soul that you are capable—because God is capable. I am here to tell you to stomp on that inner voice telling you that you can't do it. Stomp with gusto, and charge on.

At this point, you are probably wondering who I am and why I think I can tell you to listen more intently for God's calls. As a perpetual non-listener myself, I'm speaking this message to my own soul as I share it with you. In the spirit of self-reflection, as I piece together all of the intricate and jagged puzzle pieces of my life, I can see how beautiful God has made living.

I am a Christian, mama of two beautiful souls, a social worker, and the military spouse of an active duty Coast Guardsman. The last puzzle piece, as a spouse of an active duty military member, defined me for so long—and in such a deep way—that everything I did was wrapped in putting my husband's service to this country first. My ideas and vision for my life took a backseat, and it was okay—until it suddenly wasn't.

You know that overwhelming place of loss, and the guilt that comes with frustration? It feels like having a weight on your chest and an intuition that something drastically important is missing. Having this inkling doesn't mean you are ungrateful for your blessings. It just means you know there's something more you are meant for.

In January of 2019, the unpredictability of government shutdowns rendered our Coast Guard community completely without pay. Because of the shutdown, and the fact that the Coast Guard does not fall underneath the Department of Defense, all of the funding to support Coast Guardsman, along with all of the other organizations that fell under the Department of Homeland Security, were frozen. This left our community devastated. Families were left without food. New couples found themselves unable to pay their bills. It was a living nightmare.

Little did I know that within this dark and troublesome season, my mission and purpose would be revealed. Something inside told me I absolutely had to do something to help take care of our unpaid families. That voice led to me creating a massive food and supply pantry that served not only our unpaid Coast Guard families in New Jersey, but families throughout the country. I had complete faith in the project, and because I did, our families had been utilizing a pantry and saving their money long before we missed our first paycheck.

Do you know that saying "God will provide"? He will, but it helps if you hear Him so you don't miss His provision. In listening to His voice, calling me forward in obedience, not only was I able to feel His presence in the midst of madness, but He answered the prayers of so many in need.

What does that mean? God deeply loves us all and is continually lighting the way to provide for us. But if we don't believe in that light and follow it, it's lost. I am reminded of the part of the Bible that says: *Every test that you have experienced is the kind that normally comes to people. But God keeps his promise and he will not allow you to be tested beyond your power to remain firm; at the time you are put to the test, He will give you the strength to endure it, and so provide you with a way out"* (1 Corinthians 10:13, Good News Bible).

For me, this means to remain steadfast in your faith and follow the light, even when it's hard.

I won't sugar coat it. The mission God called me to wasn't pretty or easy in any way. I was beyond exhausted, over-caffeinated, and my plate was more than overflowing. During this mission (which I devoted up to ten hours a day to), I was still serving my family as a military wife, mama, and student, while working part-time. This mission challenged everything in my life. Friendships were tested and lost, and even my own marriage was negatively impacted. Through all of this, I never wavered. I knew I was doing exactly what I was meant to do.

The shutdown ended in February, and in March of 2019, I was named the Armed Forces Insurance Coast Guard Spouse of the Year. Although I didn't do the things I did for this award, it opened doors and gave me a seat at tables I would never have been invited to before. Listening to God's call and staying my course, even when I felt broken, changed the trajectory of my entire life.

My experience during the shutdown made me realize that I can be a good wife, mother, and also do what I know God is calling me to do. Every time I trusted Him, the pages in the story of my life became richer, deeply meaningful, and fulfilling. But I had to not only hear His voice guiding me towards my mission, I also had to trust it even when it hurt. Sometimes missions come during the midst of overwhelming pain. The kind of pain that leaves you breathless and aching with every fiber of your being in grief. My next call brought me there.

My grandmother was everything to me. Losing her in June of 2019, shortly after experiencing so much joy, brought me to a dark and deeply hurtful place. Life without her wasn't something I was prepared for. I vehemently disliked hearing from others that there was a reason for everything. I do believe each piece of our pain can provide an opportunity for a lesson, one that you will learn and grow from, but in my grief, all such thoughts were unwelcomed. In my heart I knew my grandmother was sick, but I was too hurt to accept that her death was a merciful gift from God—or could provide any benefit.

Before my grandmother died, I had worked hard to fundraise and find a special Coast Guard family to bring a home makeover to. I had partnered with the 2019 Army Spouse of the Year, Maria Reed, on this project. Four days after my grandmother went to heaven, my phone rang. Drowning in sorrow, I answered the call while still in my bed.

The caller said, "We have a Coast Guardsman's wife in hospice, she's terminal with cancer. His shipmates want to nominate him because he's been caring for her and their two children for four years while she's battled, and his home needed a lot of work. It's work he can't complete under the circumstances."

This was a mission from God, I just knew it. I also knew it was God's way of getting me out of that bed and carrying me through my pain.

I spent the month in between that call and the makeover reveal writing about my grandmother's life and planning for the home renovation. Interestingly, the recipient Coast Guard family lived just an hour from my grandmother's home.

We revealed the makeover, then the following day, I went to my grandmother's funeral. The mission God called me to brought me through my grief and reaffirmed my belief that I was meant to do things to help others. I promised myself right then and there that I would answer future opportunities, because I had complete faith in what I was being called to do.

I did not complete the mission by my "self," but by Him. There was no other explanation to account for why I was called home to serve a family so close to where I said my goodbye to my grandmother, only a day after I finished the project. I know she watched and loved every moment of the makeover reveal. God gave me a gift in the midst of my hurt, He trusted me with a special purpose and infused me with the strength to say goodbye.

The Merriam-Webster's definition of faith is an allegiance to a duty or a person in someone and complete trust. Personally, I like the Bible's definition better. Scripture tells us: *To have faith is to be sure of the things we hope for, to be certain of the things we cannot see* (Hebrews 11:1, Good News Bible).

Your dreams and ideas won't always come with blindingly obvious signs that they will be successful. Some of my greatest failures have offered pathways to dreams I never thought I would achieve. Sometimes you are meant to fail because the lessons you learn will lead you to something beautiful—your true mission. So when you hurt, look for the lesson in your circumstance, and your mission becomes possible.

Even in the midst of great pain, everything I have said yes to has led to incredible things. On a whim, I shared the Coast Guard makeover Maria and I did with GivingTuesday, an organization that for seven years has made the Tuesday after Thanksgiving a global day of generosity. In 2018, they raised 400 million dollars for nonprofits.

> SOMETIMES YOU ARE MEANT TO FAIL BECAUSE THE LESSONS YOU LEARN WILL LEAD YOU TO SOMETHING BEAUTIFUL—YOUR TRUE MISSION.

The GivingTuesday leaders loved what we did for our Coast Guard family and asked if we would consider running a campaign for GivingTuesday. Almost all of their campaigns are run by nonprofits and based around fundraising. We weren't feeling excited about sitting down and figuring out what it would look like and how we could honor their request. But I set the meeting anyway, not knowing what our campaign would be, and practicing faith in the mission.

Maria and I brought on our close friend, Samantha Gomolka, (she was the National Guard Spouse of the Year for 2019) for the meeting. She said yes before she even knew exactly what we were going to do. That's faith and love.

About ten minutes before our conference call started, it came to us, we knew what we wanted to do. Our entire campaign would be based on one thing: kindness. Our goal would be to activate our military networks, their families, and patriotic supporters to complete one million acts of kindness.

Kindness is the root of all that is good and right. The Bible says: *You are the people of God; he loved you and chose you for his own. So then, you must clothe yourselves with compassion, kindness, humility, gentleness, and patience* (Colossians 3:12, Good News Bible).

This passage says it all right there, be kind. Not only does the Bible instruct us to be kind, but multiple published scientific studies have proven that kindness lights our brains up like Christmas trees with all of the feel-good hormones. The happiness a giver experiences far outweighs what the person receiving the gift feels.

We knew that one act of kindness would have a ripple effect, impacting so many. Our hope was that it would change the world, and it did. We reached not just 1 million people with acts of kindness, but 2.5 million. It was a mission that started with a call to action, but above all, it required faith. And we were not finished yet.

A month later, the three of us, alongside our good friend Stacy Bilodeau (who was the 2018 Coast Guard Spouse of the Year) formed a nonprofit. GivingTuesdayMilitary made us realize we wanted to live this purpose and mission every single day. Our hope was to encourage the world to live a life of generosity and kindness, which is why we called it *Inspire Up*.

Our goal is to inspire a wave of generosity, making an undeniable social impact.

Let me tell you, starting out the process wasn't easy. I had a lot of self-doubt about starting a nonprofit in the midst of working, being a mom, and finishing graduate school. Sometimes, I felt so sick to my stomach with fear that I was on the brink of saying, "We can't do this."

A passage in the Bible reminded me of a promise I could grip. *When I am afraid, O LORD Almighty, I put my trust in you* (Psalms 56:3 Good News Bible).

Holding onto that Psalm, every time the voice of self-doubt crept in, I ignored it. Instead, I put my complete faith in God that I was on the right path. My mission was clear, and I was ready.

So, what is your mission? Mine has always started with a voice inside nudging me and a deep feeling that I was meant to do a particular thing weighing on my heart. Look at the signs all around you, and above all else, pray for God's guidance. *He gives me new strength. He guides me in the right paths, as he has promised* (Psalms 23:3 Good News Bible).

Know that some missions will feel more painful to navigate than others. That's okay—God will love you through the hard parts and fuel your strength. I believe with my whole heart that He leads us to where we need to be, even when we feel lost. But first, we have to have complete faith in Him, the mission, and ourselves. Kindness begins with belief.

(See Jessica Manfre's bio in Chapter Two)

Chapter Twenty-Five
IN THE MOMENT

SHERRY EIFLER

J**UST DO WHAT** you know to do." The Army trains with that expectation, but in the moment, I wasn't in the Army.

This is what ran through my mind as I transitioned from Captain Sherry Eifler to Army wife, Sherry Eifler. The question is, as warrior wives, how do we learn what to do in the moment? Apart from the village needed to raise a child, it takes a diligent faith community, whether inside or outside the military boundary, to prepare us for crucial moments.

Faith seeds had been planted throughout my whole life, yet left uncultivated. But once I experienced an authentic faith community, I learned how to cultivate the dormant seeds of hope in my lonely heart.

I was in transition, desperate to fill the unexpected void of living on post for the first time. A gentle knock interrupted the lazy day of this now pregnant Army wife. I opened the door to a fragrant spring day in Georgia, and was unexpectantly welcomed by my backdoor neighbor, Peggy. It struck me as unusual. I had never been welcomed in my civilian neighborhoods.

Peggy extended a warm, freshly baked loaf of bread and invited me to join Protestant Women of the Chapel (PWOC). But I was a hard sell. Why did I need PWOC? I already had spouse training to guide me in my new role as an Army wife.

Peggy was a warrior wife though, and she won me over with authentic connection, and an offer of friendship. But her invitation was not a singular event. She asked me to join her when she went to pick blueberries. When she visited her other local favorites, she asked if I'd like to come. She had me over for dinners with her family. And she even allowed me to watch her young boys on occasion. Peggy was genuine and not willing to give up on me.

Soon, she followed up with another invitation to PWOC, and this time I went. To be honest, it wasn't what I expected. I didn't really fit right in right away, but I gave it a chance because I had grown to know and like Peggy. I trusted that this must be a place worthy of exploration, though it took years before I realized the full impact of the warrior wives who surrounded me.

PWOC became my trusted community, my sisterhood that linked hearts and arms with me at each new duty station. Their life-changing influence prepared me for many of life's moments. I embraced the faith and learned how to be ready in the moment. I became a warrior wife in my own right, as a prayer, community service person, leader, marriage partner, parent, and friend. I was ready in the moment when deployment called, tragedy interrupted, trauma terrorized, and sickness held me down. My PWOC sisters taught me to trust God, so I knew how to lean on Him when I need help most.

As you read this, you might wonder: *What does trusting God look like? I want to, but I'm not sure if my concerns even matter to Him.* Let me give you an example from my own life.

We had just returned from an amazing surprise family trip to Disney World. Joyful exhaustion filled our hearts and bodies as we settled back into our routine. Arriving home from a trip to the grocery store, we found a red Jeep parked and waiting for us in the driveway. It was like a pin popped my joy balloon. The last time we saw a red Jeep at our house, it wasn't good news.

The messenger in the Jeep said my husband had to return from leave immediately.

I unloaded the groceries, the kids played, and my husband transitioned from daddy to soldier—then off he went. I watched him follow the red Jeep down the street.

Hours later, children sleeping, my husband finally returned. I wasn't sure how to interpret his body language. Then he spoke. His words left me feeling frozen in time.

"I'm being deployed to Iraq. The timeframe isn't clear, so I'm not sure how long I'll be gone."

The next day after packing, my husband left to oversee equipment loading. We weren't sure if he would get to come back home before leaving with the ship.

My Army training kicked in. I knew what he had to do, and I knew this meant I needed to put my Ranger Wife armor on. This wasn't the first time my soldier was called up in a moment's notice, but it would be my first time as a mom of a six-year-old, three-year-old, and almost two-year-old. My faith community had taught me what to do—I turned to God, trusted him, and leaned on my PWOC sisterhood.

The send-off ceremony is still a blur in my mind. What I do remember is that it was two days before my birthday. During our final embrace, my husband held me tight and spoke optimism. He whispered, "I will see you in six months, my love."

My response, a surprise to both of us was, "I will see you by my next birthday, my love."

The look he gave me. "Sherry, what do you mean?"

"I don't know. I just believe that came from the Lord. Hold onto it, it will anchor us through the unknown desert ahead."

Three months later, when his unit's time overseas was extended, the Lord's anchor of truth held us steady and secure. It also allowed us to help others through the uncertainty and disappointment of an unknown future.

During that deployment, I experienced an unexplainable deepening of my connection within my faith community. As my soldier was heading to battle, the Lord was establishing this warrior wife in leadership, as the local PWOC president. The Lord used every facet of my godly relationships to meet the needs He knew I had before I even experienced them.

> **THE LORD USED EVERY FACET OF MY GODLY RELATIONSHIPS TO MEET THE NEEDS HE KNEW I HAD BEFORE I EVEN EXPERIENCED THEM.**

On-post chapel families adopted our families, those with deployed soldiers, to assist us at home. PWOC sisters watched my children, helped as needed, and prayed with and for us. These warriors for the faith loved on my family in many selfless ways, including when even tougher times hit.

My husband was still deployed, so my parents were coming to visit and watch the kids while I attended a PWOC training conference. I was a workshop presenter, so it was important that I go. The night before flying to the conference, my dad was admitted to the hospital and I was left wondering, *should I stay, or should I go?*

I talked to my dad, a strong man of faith, and his words pierced my heart. "Sherry you are going. I will be fine—this is your time."

In that moment, I knew I must choose to trust God, so I did. And He sent His warrior angels, once again. They swooped in and took over watching the kids and getting them to school, while caring for my mom and dad in a strange town and hospital. They even dropped me off at the airport. How do you ever express your gratitude to the fullest after being blessed like that?

I believe the best way to express gratitude for someone's kindness and love is to pass it on. So, here's a challenge. Will you choose to pass on your blessings, as my diligent faith community members and warrior angels did?

There are so many more "Sherrys" out there, either in transition or in one of life's difficult seasons, waiting for their invitation to friendship, and who want to learn how to trust God. This offers you an opportunity. Together, we can raise warrior wives—women who are equipped, educated, and experienced to trust God. This is your moment to make all of your other moments count. What will you do with yours?

(See Sherry Eifler's bio in Chapter Twelve)

Chapter Twenty-Six
WHERE TWO OR MORE ARE GATHERED

AJ SMIT

"For where two or three gather in my name, there I am with them"
MATTHEW 18:20 NIV

CHRIST MADE US this promise. Sadly, we forget the scale of that promise. We go big—we go to mega-churches, we count our followers, or we measure the success of our ministry by the number of seats filled. The promise is "two or three," a small gathering. I sometimes forget that the little, everyday things we overlook fall under that promise, too.

As women, we feel called to create and be in friendship, and this is good. But, we ought to remember that "gathering" can take many forms. We believe, as I did, that a good gathering means spreading ourselves thin to bring together friends and family in big, splashy events: Thanksgiving tables laden with food, Instagram-worthy birthday parties, or note-perfect funerals. However, I've learned the important times to gather are often in the quiet moments that sometimes slip by. In these moments, we need to help our friends pull themselves together and be willing to sit with open arms, tears streaming. This is my story of how I was called to remember a smaller kind of gathering.

My life revolves around women. In our Red Tent, we congregate together once a month, on or near the new moon, to talk about periods, our cycles, rape, miscarriage, birth, authentic womanhood, boundaries, and more. We talk about the big stuff and go deep, priding ourselves on showing up for each other when the going gets rough. Our Tent has hosted art nights, potlucks, and even weekend-long retreats.

Recently, after we had finished our last retreat, we stood in the tiny parking lot, giving each other hugs before turning our phones on and driving back into the real world. One of our women said, "She lost Mace."

We didn't believe it at first. Ashley was due in two weeks. The only reason she didn't attend the retreat was because she was picking up her mom at the airport. She wasn't supposed to be giving birth or doing anything more than waddling awkwardly. She wasn't supposed to be in the hospital. But she had lost her baby, Mace, two weeks before her due date.

Sudden infant loss shouldn't be a real thing. Those heartbreaking stories were just old wives' tales, right? With the aid of modern medicine, it should have been smooth sailing after week twelve. But here we were, crashing from an exquisite weekend into reality, where all of our worst nightmares had come true.

In the movies, you see sobbing. You hear about women wailing at the wall, or women crying out at a sudden loss. But as awareness of Ashley's loss washed over us, I had a new understanding of what "wailing" actually meant. Yet, it still did not cover the truth of how we felt.

One of our core members, Elissa, gathered us together to pray and send love, uniting our grief and channeling it to give Ashley our hope and our strength. Roles were assigned—one woman went to the hospital, and another was put in charge of figuring out what Ashley's family needed, and organizing a meal train. The Tent had it covered. As a group, we gathered in unity around her in her time of crisis, but my special efforts were not needed. The rest of our team had it covered. They went where they were needed. I went home and slept.

I didn't want to overstep and crowd in to help, so I stayed back. I didn't reach out directly to Ashley, because what do you say? I assumed Ashley wouldn't want someone awkwardly sitting on her couch. I was quiet. I can organize a group of twenty women to share their feelings, but how do I contribute or add value when I don't have a lesson plan? I wasn't sure. I decided I'd rather give a grieving woman space and hope it would be helpful, than risk the chance of overcrowding her. At least that's what I told myself.

There are miscarriage rituals—old, sacred evenings to honor the mother, the baby, to grieve the possibilities that never had a chance to flourish. I had heard of them, but we had never done one before. As leader of our Tent, I threw myself into this one way I could serve. I messaged Ashley to assist in planning her evening.

The ceremony was beautiful and heart-wrenching. She shared pictures, told her womb story. We lit candles, sobbed, laughed, ate chocolate, and cried some more. I felt I had done my part in helping her by planning and hosting this one Big Thing. It was safer in my mind to create and hold a Big Space than to be present in a small space.

When I told my mom about Ashley's miscarriage, she said she'd like to send her some things. She found a book and stuffed animal for Ashley's toddler, and a CD from a Christian lady who had a miscarriage. Ashley didn't share our same faith, so I told my mom that if she really wanted to send it, I'd ask Ashley if she was interested. I was more afraid of offending her as she mourned than concerned about how I could show up for her in any way possible.

I sent the care package to one of the three women who brought Ashley food, and passed along my fears of it being too much. I told them I didn't want to overstep Ashley's faith with "Christian-ese how to grieve 101." I had confided this with nervousness. The woman passed the goods, and my disclaimer on to Ashley.

Ashley adored the care package. Her son loved the book and stuffed animal. Ashley deeply appreciated the CD. From a distant place, my mom showed up to support my friend in a small, intimate way for someone she'd never met before in an offering of love. I was afraid to do the same. I thought it would mean the most to Ashley if I showed up during the Big Evening, doing the thing I was best at.

Don't get me wrong, the Big Evening was good, needed even, but in that care package, I saw that the small things are important, too. For me, small things are the scarier of the two. When you can feel the nerves at the edge of your skin, having no words to mend anything, only arms to offer in embrace, I get uncomfortable. I can do the Big Gathering, but the small type of gathering—those make it or break it tiny moments of friendship—that's another story.

At our following Red Tent, Ashley pulled me into the kitchen, and said, "I know you were nervous about sending me your mom's items. But babe, never be afraid to show love."

This sentence shook me to my core. Tears streamed down my face. as Ashley fiercely hugged me. And I realized that this, too, was gathering. She was bringing me back to who we are as women. We can often miss opportunities to show up in small and large ways for our loved ones and friends.

Ashley and I were both part of a Red Tent. I was the main leader, and she had a miscarriage a month prior. In that hug, she helped me remember the potency of showing up for each other with grace and compassion.

In that hug, I realized gathering isn't just events or a specific evening set aside for ceremony. While it can be that, gathering can also mean sitting on someone's couch and talking about life, going for a walk at night with them, sending someone a letter in the mail, or making a call when someone pops into your mind. Gathering in friendship can mean listening to the divine nudge God gives you and obeying the small whisper. "Go talk to them. Go tell them I love them. Go love them well."

IN THAT HUG, I REALIZED GATHERING ISN'T JUST EVENTS OR A SPECIFIC EVENING SET ASIDE FOR CEREMONY.

It's scary, this small form of gathering. You don't want to screw it up, get it wrong, or say the inappropriate thing. You want to show up in the right way, not to overstep boundaries, but to also say you will be with them to weather the difficult times. I don't know how life will look for any of us tomorrow. But I know this—when you show up, willing to give love, authentically with your hands open, even when afraid and trembling—that's what true gathering and friendship is all about.

(See AJ Smit's bio in Chapter Eleven)

Chapter Twenty-Seven
FAITH UNFOLDED

CHANDEE ULCH

WALKED INTO THE house boiling with frustration. I went into the living room, where my parents sat watching television. I plopped on the couch and tried to make it obvious I wanted to talk. I looked at my mom and said, "You won't believe what they asked me to do at the Bible Study tonight."

"What did they ask?"

"They want me to share my testimony next week."

"Okay, I'm not sure why you are upset about it."

"Because I don't have a testimony, and it is all your fault. You and Dad made it where I don't have a testimony."

"Chandee, how did your dad and I make it where you don't have a testimony?" Mom said. Her face mirrored the puzzled sound in her voice.

By now, I had the attention of both my parents and my youngest brother.

I am one of three children. I'm the oldest, and the only girl, which means for the first five years of my life my parents poured their loves and passions into me. My mother likes creating, and she gave me a love for creating. I use this gift in my photography, videography, crafts, storytelling, and more. My father liked martial arts and Bruce Lee movies, and I still love watching those old films. But above all, both my parents loved Christ. Church was like a second home for us. And, yes, they laid the foundation for my relationship with Jesus.

Christ for me was always like breathing oxygen, He was just there. I honestly cannot remember a time in life when Jesus Christ wasn't real. Accepting Jesus as my Lord and Savior felt more like a formality at age five than anything else. My father has always said he learned something new about God through each of his children. From me, he learned childlike faith. Growing up with no doubt that Jesus Christ was and is God Almighty made me question if I had anything to share with anyone.

"Mom, you came to know the Lord when you were in your teens. So, you remember life without having a relationship with Christ. You've said life without Him was black, and now that you know Him, life is white. I don't have the black and white story. I don't have a story at all. I have never questioned if there was a God. I have always known He was there. How is it a testimony?"

My dad decided it was time to interject, "Chandee, I know what you are going through. Like you, I accepted Christ at a young age. But the truth is, no matter how young or old you are, each of us have a testimony, because each of us have to work out our own salvation. And I have seen you do it for years now."

My father was right, of course—aren't all dads right? (Shh! Don't tell him I ever said that). I sat next to my parents, reminiscing about the past five years. No, I never questioned if there was a God, or if He was Jesus Christ. But I did question His plan for my life.

As a teenager, I struggled with God because He made me different, and I didn't want to be different. Typical to most teens, being different felt like a curse. I felt as though I was always walking a tightrope, trying to get as close to the world as I could, while crying myself asleep at night, knowing in my heart I was wrong. For many years, I chose to believe the lies the world said about me. I allowed those lies to seep into my spirit so deeply, it left intense wounds.

Over time and with God's grace, He has healed many of those wounds. But some wounds leave scars. The scar of writing is one I'm struggling with, even as I share my message with you now.

The voice of an old English teacher lingers in my head, "Chandee, change your dreams. You will never be able to do it." She told me this during the first week of school.

When I was in second grade (the first time), I had a teacher who told me it was a good thing I was friendly, because I should get married young. She thought I would never be able to finish school.

By sixth grade, they put me in a class with other special-need students—some had Downs Syndrome and cerebral palsy. With God's compassion, those students became some of my dear friends.

In high school, teachers pushed me through each grade. And when graduation came, they realized I was barely reading at a fifth-grade level. Having dyslexia, and a school system that didn't know how to help me, meant I spent many years feeling as though I was a failure. I believed I was never going to amount to anything. Those lies left many scars on my spirit.

I've learned that every day, I have to make a choice to believe what God says about me over what the world has said. Yet, the world seems to yell its lies, while God's truth comes in a whisper. *Why?*

I once challenged a teacher on this topic, "Teacher, it is so much easier to hear the yelling of the world than the whispers of God."

She chose not to respond to my statement in the moment. But the next day, she brought a beautiful landscape photo with luscious mountainside and valleys shining through a sunset. The image was spectacular. She asked me, "What do you notice first in this image?"

I'VE LEARNED THAT EVERY DAY, I HAVE TO MAKE A CHOICE TO BELIEVE WHAT GOD SAYS ABOUT ME, OVER WHAT THE WORLD HAS SAID.

"The stop sign," I said.

Then, she set the poster down and started teaching the class.

At the end of class, I raised my hand and asked, "Teacher, what was the point in you asking me the question about the poster?"

"I am glad you asked. This image is in black and white. It is a landscape image. Ninety-nine percent of the image is beautiful scenery. The scenery yells at you. It is screaming at you to look at it, and you are. And yet, when I asked you to pick out the first thing you noticed, you chose the word *STOP*. Words are powerful. Words demand our attention. Words draw our eyes. Humans are curious creatures, and when we see words, we need to know what they say—it is human nature. This is why God gave us His Word. He knew the world would yell at us. The screaming in our spirit would come from every direction. But His Word would be more powerful than any yelling. The only thing we have to do is open it up. Our eyes will be drawn to it. Our attention will be curious, and our spirit will want to know it. All we have to do is *STOP* and read it."

I've come to realize my testimony isn't about coming to faith. My testimony is about taking my faith and walking in trust. Trusting God with my questions, wounds, struggles, and doubts. It is a trek I am still walking on with God. He exposes lies from wounds in the past and then spends time, sometimes years, healing me with His truth.

I worked through my testimony with my parents the next week. Not only did God show me He has given me things to share with others, but He chose to show me in my living room. After I finished talking with my parents, my youngest brother, Chase, looked at me and said, "Chandee, I have never done it."

"What haven't you done?"

"I have never asked Jesus into my heart."

That night, with a testimony I thought I never had, I listened to my brother, as he gave his life to the Lord. He chose to put his faith in Jesus Christ. Sometimes, faith unfolds right before our eyes.

(See Chandee Ulch's bio in Chapter Nine)

Part Six

CUT FROM THE SAME CLOTH: THE WARRIOR WOMEN

Chapter Twenty-Eight
FINDING PURPOSE AGAIN

AMANDA HUFFMAN

IF SOMEONE HAD told me how drastically my life would change when I left the military after being connected to it for over ten years, I would have rolled my eyes. As an officer in the Air Force, I saw combat in Afghanistan, led men and women, and was responsible for millions of dollars of construction projects. Psssh, being a stay-at-home mom to one kid and a military spouse? Walk in the park, right?

It only took a few weeks for me to realize how completely naive I was.

I joined ROTC my sophomore year of college with the goal of becoming a second lieutenant in the Air Force. Sure enough, four years later, I graduated college with a degree in Civil Engineering and gold bars on my shoulders. I was so focused on commissioning I almost missed the importance and accomplishment of earning my degree.

Serving in the Air Force was ingrained into my purpose, yet I came close to losing it all due to a medical evaluation. It almost cost me my commission. I instantly became blinded to all of my other achievements over the past four years of college.

So, is it any wonder that when I left the military behind to become a mom and military spouse, I had a major identity crisis?

All of a sudden, the certainty I felt in my identity was stripped away from me. My ten years of confident purpose disappeared. Previously, I knew who I was and where I was going, even if the military had total control. It didn't matter that I didn't actually know where I would be living in a year or the location of my service. I knew who I was, and why I was there. This passion burned inside of me. My military service got me out of bed and told me I was worthy, strong, and valuable, until I took my uniform off for the last time. Instantly, my assurance was gone. I felt lost.

It was as if the ground under me unraveled and I couldn't find my footing. I didn't know who I was or where I was going. I felt like I was free-falling, scrambling to find myself. I tried transferring my sense of purpose and belonging to something greater than myself—in my new role as a mom. But I had no idea that what I imagined as easy, would prove one of the hardest endeavors of my life.

I didn't realize that transformation would come with time and a lot of struggle along the way. Isn't motherhood something you are hardwired to do? I had an advantage, after all. Self-sacrifice was something I had learned in the military. I knew what it meant to give my all to someone else, as I did every day for the men and women I served with. But when it came to being a mom, I felt lost and overwhelmed. No one seemed to notice the work I was doing. No one was measuring or awed by how many diapers I changed or how many hours of sleep I missed. The only person constantly with me was my baby. My perfectionistic personality told me I was failing. Each day, I counted my every flaw and berated myself for falling short from the perfect mom I had dreamed of being.

Becoming a mom, especially when you choose the path of leaving your career dreams, requires you to break up with your old self. And that process is painful. It took me years to answer the question: *Was leaving the military behind the right choice?*

For so long, my answer focused on a rose-colored world. Remembering the direction I once had for my life versus floundering and rediscovering what I was meant to do next, I felt stuck and unfocused. I couldn't stop thinking about what I had given up. I wished I could go back to a time when things felt simple and clear.

> **I WENT FROM THE DRIVER'S SEAT OF MY LIFE TO BEING SENT TO THE BACK OF THE CAR.**

The challenges of why I left the military were forgotten, and instead replaced with a dream-like reality.

Deep down, I knew leaving the military and becoming a stay-at-home mom and military spouse was the right choice. But it was so hard to make the transition. I went from the driver's seat of my life to being sent to the back of the car. My husband's career now drove my existence. The military cared nothing about my goals, wishes, and dreams.

That was the hardest part of transitioning. When I left the military behind, I hadn't realized the gambit of sacrifices military spouses must make. Even though they were not the ones who signed up to serve, the military makes a huge impact on their lives. They have zero say in those decisions.

When I was in the Air Force, I was consulted. My career mattered just as much as my husband's. As a milspouse, I was forgotten and invisible in a place I had once stood out.

Over time, my struggle with the military led me to resent

my veteran status and hide away the part inside of me I had once been so proud of. I did not join veteran organizations and instead only identified with my new role as spouse—even if I wasn't sure what it all meant. I became active in the military spouse community and wore my title boldly.

But still, I felt this pull to share stories of those who had served in the armed forces. It was the thread that continually pulled me back. I tried to hide it away, until a voice from a stranger said, "But I think your experience as a veteran is interesting and I want to learn more."

This gave me pause.

So, I took the bait and started collecting true stories of deployments. As I searched for accounts from anyone sent out for duty, I found women. Women willing and ready to share their military experience with me. I ended up with a deployment series primarily focused on what women went through, and it switched a light on inside myself.

I wondered if I could still have an impact in this world. Maybe my military service was just part of the story, and there was more story to tell. Maybe the passion I had wasn't dead, but instead redirected.

As I continued collecting the stories of military women, I began to hear from more and more who served at different times, in different career fields, and in different branches. I discovered a place of healing and a place of belonging for myself. I slowly began to unpack that identity I had hidden away.

Today, as I speak to each female for my podcast, *Women of the Military*, these conversations help me realize I am not alone. And even though I may not be recognized by the general public for the service I am doing as a mother, I can do something important and I can make a change. I don't have to serve in the military to fulfill a calling bigger than myself. I can share the stories of women who have served, and details people never get to hear, by using my voice as a platform to elevate the voices of others.

I can now proudly answer the question, *Did I make the right choice in leaving the military when my son was born?*

Yes! I was made to not only be a mom and military spouse, but also to influence the world by sharing the stories of military women. And I can do all of this while finding the right balance between work, motherhood, and being a wife. And if I hadn't left the military behind, I might never have found the three roles that make up my life's ultimate calling.

I sacrificed what I was most proud of to become a mom, but I gained so much more through the experience of transitioning out of the military, and to the woman I am today. It wasn't easy. There were a lot of missteps and course corrections along the way. But when I look at who I am now, I am so thankful for the journey, because it brought me to where I am.

I am proud to be a mom, a military spouse, *and* a veteran.

AMANDA is a military spouse and veteran who served in the Air Force for six years as a Civil Engineer, deploying to Afghanistan. She met her husband while attending college, and they served on active duty until the birth of their son. Then, she traded her combat boots for a diaper bag as a Stay-at-Home Mom. Amanda is now a mother of two boys and faithfully follows her husband's military career. She has been stationed in New Mexico, Ohio, and California. She currently resides in North Virginia with her family. Her first book, *Women of the Military*, shares the story of 28 women who served on active duty. In 2019, she also launched her "Women of the Military" podcast where she features the heroic women that have served and serve today, including the 23rd Secretary of the Air Force and Brigadier General Wilma Vaught. You can learn more about Amanda at her website www.AirmantoMom.com.

Chapter Twenty-Nine
A DREAM DEFERRED

LAURA SCHOFIELD

THIS VERSE GUIDES my life.

For my thoughts are not your thoughts, declares the Lord. For as the heavens are higher than the earth, so are my ways higher than your ways and my thoughts than your thoughts. For as the rain and the snow come down from heaven and do not return there but water the earth, making it bring forth and sprout, giving seed to the sower and bread to the eater, so shall my word be that goes out from my mouth; it shall not return to me empty, but it shall accomplish that which I purpose, and shall succeed in the thing for which I sent it. (Isaiah 55: 8-11 ESV)

The year I turned sixteen was also the year I started college, thanks to my home state's dual enrollment program. I loved my years at that community college, and the future stretched out in front of me with endless possibilities. Surrounded by friends, I thrived in my classes, and I used the exposure to so many different fields of study to discover many new interests.

When considering my plans for after college, my ideas for a career were diverse and reflected many different passions. I considered becoming a librarian, or maybe an American Sign Language interpreter, or even joining the Federal Bureau of Investigations. The military was not even a blip on my radar—it had truly never occurred to me.

I loved my criminal justice classes and decided to pursue a career with the FBI. I realized I needed qualifications that might be problematic for my current trajectory. I was on course to have my bachelor's degree by the time I was twenty, which was great for jump-starting a career, but not when the FBI required applicants to be at least twenty-three with professional experience. *How in the world was I going to get that?*

On a whim one day, I filled out a postcard for the Washington Army National Guard. I still cannot say what prompted me to do this, I barely knew what the National Guard was and joining was certainly something I had never considered before. I received a phone call from a recruiter right away, asking me to come to his office and chat about "what the National Guard could offer me." So, I went.

The seeming disparity from who I was as a person and what the military was all about was apparent even from the beginning. I wore a skirt with flowers on it to meet with the recruiter for the first time at the local National Guard Armory. But the pitch sounded good to me. I could join with an intelligence-based occupation specialty (MOS), work one weekend a month, receive college assistance, and get that "professional experience" I needed on my resume.

But at seventeen years old, I needed my parents' permission to enlist. With the National Guard, I could attend Basic Combat Training (boot camp) during the summer and return home in time to finish my last year of high school. After that, I would go to specialized schools and join a deployable unit after I turned eighteen and had my general associate's degree.

I presented my case to my parents. Despite their hesitations at sending their little girl off to boot camp, they could see that this would be a good starting point for the career I wanted. They also recognized that my desire to join the military was far outside my natural inclinations, and that the Holy Spirit was prompting me in ways I couldn't even articulate. Within a month of first meeting with the recruiter, my parents signed the permission slips, and I went to the local Military Entrance Processing Station (MEPS), signed my contract, and prepared to go to Basic Training.

While I was not overweight, I was definitely not athletically inclined. Instead, I brought high test scores and a clean record that would make obtaining a security clearance a guarantee, all attractive traits in a new recruit. I wasn't particularly concerned about my lack of skill in the push up and running department. I knew it would be a challenge for me, but my recruiter assured me that training was designed for people like me, who would need to start from the ground level in their fitness.

I made my way from Seattle to Fort Jackson, South Carolina, which was just about as different from home as any place in the United States could possibly be. I was not prepared in any way for the intense heat and humidity. I knew it would be hot. I had traveled to the East Coast on vacation before, but I had never spent so much time outdoors, exercising, and in long pants and long sleeves under the beating sun.

With many tears and exhaustion from the high temperatures, lack of sleep, and homesickness, I made it through the first few weeks. Daily morning exercise preceding an intensely physical day was entirely foreign to me. I often spent my evenings and down-time in "remedial physical training." I was always trying to get my pushup count up and work on my running.

> **I FELT THAT THE LORD HAD GIFTED ME THIS CHANCE TO HAVE THE CAREER I WANTED, AND I WAS DETERMINED TO FINISH STRONG.**

One day, my entire platoon (of about thirty-five recruits) was given a corporal punishment that included sprinting up and down stairs, alternating between running shoes and combat boots. I had experienced mild shin pain throughout training, but I shrugged it off as just getting used to exercising. After those sprints, however, mild discomfort shifted to crippling pain. In the following weeks, my injuries, diagnosed as "shin splints," became visible lumps on my legs, and made running almost an impossibility. But I had come this far. I felt that the Lord had gifted me this chance to have the career I wanted, and I was determined to finish strong.

I did. In a moment that could only have been God's hand beneath my feet, I was able to sprint my way through my final Physical Fitness Test and pass with the required time to graduate boot camp. That final run came with a price. I flew home to begin my senior year of high school, and I arrived at Sea-Tac airport with a pronounced limp and shuffle, just to self-manage the pain. I am sure it was shocking for both my parents and strangers to see this young girl in uniform, walking through the airport with every step causing me visible pain. *How was this part of the plan?*

Once I got home and slipped back into normal life, I was able to attend physical therapy. The stress fractures were not showing up on X-Rays, but the doctors knew they existed. They did their best to help me to heal. However, my obligation with the National Guard required that I run a timed two miles every month, in order to continually show I was meeting the Army's physical requirements. Every run became a one-step-forward-two-steps-back in recuperating from my injuries.

My final run at boot camp would be the one and only time I would ever meet the time standards. Month after month, the pain and lasting shin problems prevented me from ever meeting the Army's standard for its soldiers. After a year of monthly tests and training, I was given a general discharge (under honorable circumstances), and that was that. No intelligence training, and I did not qualify for any tuition assistance of any kind. It was almost as if my time with the National Guard had never happened. And yet, I was changed.

Instead of the brilliant career with the FBI I had imagined: using my interrogative skills to track down terrorists and save the world, I walked away from my dreams of government service. It had seemed so clear to me that I was *meant* to join the National Guard. *What was the point in dashed hopes and deferred dreams? How was this part of Your master plan, Lord?* Years would pass before I saw the true value of that time in my life. Deep and lasting empathy for the lowest ranks of the military would become the most cherished consequence.

My service to our country has shifted from what I had planned, to serving as the spouse of an active duty Marine. Showing empathy and using my voice to make a difference has become a profound conviction and dedication in my life. It was not my intended goal when I enlisted all those years ago, but my experiences then have become the greatest gift now. It is the privilege of my life to look into a junior enlisted service member's eyes and say, "I see you. I see your struggles. I see your hopes and dreams. I see your hesitancy to reach out for help. I see your fear. I see your hurt. I see you."

The practical tools I have learned throughout the passing years have given me more opportunities than I can count to shine the hope of Jesus into dark places. I cannot say whether or not I would have gone through with joining the National Guard if I could have foreseen the future. But I can see where my plans failed—the Lord's plans flourished. The cost I paid has been worth every tear and moment of struggle to be able to say to another, "I understand." I know the race I run as a follower of Christ has been marked for me, and I can look back with gratefulness at where He has guided me so far. His plans are truly perfect.

My mother wrote this poem for me when I left for boot camp, and the words are even more meaningful now:

"*She doesn't seek your approval,*
Her desires have been God-given,
Her path directed.
She covets your prayers, but not for what you think.
To glorify her Savior in what she does,
To be salt and light in a sea of humanity,
To be the tangible outpouring of God's grace
To those who do not know Him."
Debbie Woldstad

LAURA SCHOFIELD has been a military spouse for all of her adult life. She pulls from her family's own experiences in navigating the difficulties and joys of daily military life to come alongside others.

Laura passionately uses her voice to break the silences surrounding the struggles that military families, especially spouses, face. In between homeschooling three children, quilting, and re-decorating her vintage government housing, she can be found on Instagram @ myquietsmalllife.

Chapter Thirty
FROM SERVICE TO FINDING YOUR CALLING

MEGAN HARLESS

O**N A SHOOTING** range in West Virginia, I met my soon-to-be husband, Aaron Harless, in 2003. We were paired together on the firing line for an exercise and I remember thinking, *Wow, he is cute.* Two weeks later, we started dating. I was a biology Pre-Med major at the University of Charleston in West Virginia. He was enrolled as a Criminal Justice student at West Virginia State University, about fifteen minutes away from my campus. The ROTC (Reserve Officer Training Corp) program was combined for our two campuses.

I had an iron clad plan to finish my pre-med requirements at UCWV and then go to P.A. School. Needless to say, that all changed because of a gorgeous man in uniform. We got married in 2005, two days before Christmas in the middle of a blizzard.

It's funny how a man in uniform can derail the best laid strategy with little more than a smile and a proposal.

Two years later, when my husband left for his first deployment in 2007, I was twelve weeks pregnant with our first child. That night, I laid awake inside of our on-post home, holding my slightly swollen belly. I soaked my pillow with tears as my husband traveled overseas to join the troop surge to Iraq. Ultimately, we spent over fifteen months apart. This deployment set the stage for the rest of our joint military experience.

Time continued on, and in 2009, I commissioned into the Unites States Army as a Second Lieutenant. We also found out we would soon have another baby. I was nine weeks pregnant when my husband vanished again to serve in his second deployment. At the time, I was living out of a suitcase in a hotel, because I was attending my Transportation Basic Officer Leaders Course in Fort Eustis. Little did I know, a harder season was on the horizon.

By the third time my husband deployed, we had been married for six years, served on dual military orders (both of us were active duty soldiers), and our oldest child was about to turn four. Our youngest was only sixteen months old.

In 2011, my husband and I moved our two children into my husband's old bedroom at my in-laws home as we prepared for our deployment brigade again. This time, we were both scheduled to ship out. The initial shutdown of Iraq was commencing.

During our scheduled 12-month deployment, we had planned for my husband's parents to take care of our boys. At their house, our kids would have stability in who was caring for them and we knew they would be loved. We could trust that they would be given everything they needed in our absence. Having to drive away from my sons was one of the hardest things that I have ever had to do in my life.

As I looked in the rear-view mirror, I saw my sons standing on the porch, eyes filled with tears, as they waved "goodbye." My chest tightened as I wondered if they would be okay. Thoughts began flooding my mind. *Would I ever see them again? What happens if I don't come home?* Driving away felt like I was leaving my heart behind after it was ripped from out of my chest.

Aaron had deployed a few days before me with his battalion, and once in Iraq, would head to a different area from my assignment. We would be separated.

At the time, soldiers entering Iraq passed through Kuwait on their way north. From there, they caught transport to their new duty stations. Being in Kuwait seemed strange at first. It was the place where my husband had been in transition when I told him we were expecting our second child, and where he learned our son had been born early.

> **A CALMING SENSE OF PEACE FLOODED MY SOUL. THERE WAS SENSE OF SOMETHING BIGGER THAN ME AT WORK. I KNEW I COULD TRUST GOD WAS WITH ME *AND* MY CHILDREN.**

Kuwait was this far-off place I had only seen pictures of and heard stories about. And now, here I was walking the sandy streets between our tent and the dining facility. It felt surreal.

During the few short days spent there, I felt as if something happened to me. A shift took place. A calming sense of peace flooded my soul. There was sense of something bigger than me at work. I knew I could trust God was with me *and* my children.

Somewhere between Kuwait and Iraq, a Scripture from the Lord was planted firmly in my heart. Jeremiah 29:11 (NLT) *"For I know the plans I have for you, says the Lord,"* started playing on repeat inside of me. It's uncanny to think back on it, but from that moment, I knew that if something were to happen to me on that deployment, my boys would be okay. They would have what they needed, and as their lives went on, they would be taken care of.

When I arrived in Iraq, it felt like "go time" from the moment we rolled into our COS (Combat Operational Site). We were thrust into the handover from the previous unit, and immediately set up our operations. Meetings plagued my agenda as I was the Battalion Maintenance Officer (BMO). I was responsible for ensuring our equipment stayed operationally ready. I was also tasked with seeing that our systems for maintenance, repair, and recovery were up and running smoothly.

The undisclosed location where I was stationed was small. The perimeter wall cramped us into a physically meager space, void of places to seek respite or comfort. I saw the same people every day. I did the same activities. It felt a little bit like *Ground Hog's Day*, where I took the same steps as the day before, waiting for life to start new again.

At times, it felt overwhelmingly lonely. All the while, God repeatedly spoke into my soul, *"For I know the plans I have for you."*

These words echoed through me when I made the trek from my sleep quarters to the motor pool. And on the few times I left the COS on a convoy or in a Blackhawk, He whispered that comforting message. The times we sat in bunkers through indirect fire, God's promise *"For I know the plans I have for you,"* kept me focused on what needed to happen, even though I had no idea what the bigger plans were.

The following months were an emotional roller coaster, because there was no semblance of detailed strategy. Even the plans in the works changed rapidly. Because we were there to exit Iraq and close down operating stations, the timeline and events involved were unclear. I wondered: *When we finish, will we be al-*

lowed to return home? Or because we are on 12-month deployment orders, will our interim time be spent in Kuwait? No one knew.

I left Iraq on Thanksgiving Day and we ended up in Kuwait for the remainder of our stint in the Middle East. Most of our time there was spent training after the drawdown. We were also "setting the theater," meaning we would be a ready force to respond if aggressions transpired.

My husband and I were reunited geographically in Kuwait, but it proved hard on us. We no longer had small CHU's (containerized housing units), like those we occupied in Iraq, but instead, were now set up in 50-man tents, a place with no privacy. These tents felt more like jail and increased our misery after Iraq.

It was an immense struggle to be a married couple who could not be together physically. While we were in the same location, we felt like we were under a microscope and all of our interactions were being analyzed. The situation created tension and caused us to argue. The whole ordeal seemed like a trial, one that made me unsure of the outcome. But God continued imparting wisdom and invited me to trust.

Finally, my husband and I found time to talk to my battalion chaplain through a few meetings—think intensive marriage counseling. We found the words we could not find before. I saw through new lenses what it was like for my husband on his previous two deployments. We understood how our circumstances, chosen professions, the drawdown of Iraq, and the weight of our living arrangements pressured us. Instead of enjoying the effective communication we once had, the situation caused us to spit out the only words we could quickly find. But we worked through our misunderstandings and I was able to sift through my own internal struggle.

We returned home in June 2012, and eleven months later, I transitioned out of the Army. I was pregnant with the child who would complete our family. It was time for me to respond to the calling of supporting my husband and fellow military spouses.

I didn't know it then, but my military service and deployment experience empowered me to help others. I could share new perspectives, tell military spouses who were struggling through first or second deployments where they could find strength, and point others to faith. Through God's strength and His promise of a future, I was able to lay my own fears to rest. His promises proved true. They are still true for those who seek Him. On the other end of deployment and my transition out of the military, I am still finding that He "knows" the plans He has for me. He has good plans for you, too.

(See Megan Harless's bio in Chapter Three)

Chapter Thirty-One
THE GARMENTS I HAVE WORN

DANIELLE WHALEN

THERE IS NOTHING unique or outside of the human experience that you will find within the narrative of my life. Abandonment, abuse, unbearable pain from death and loss, failure, disappointment, debilitating depression and anxiety, heart-wrecking grief, paralyzing fear, self-doubt, and loathing riddle my story like bullet holes. This world has waged war on my soul, but my anecdote is not one of defeat. The time-old tale of terror experienced in this world does not get to claim me as its conquest. In fact, the only memoir of value you will find woven throughout my life is not about me specifically, but of the garments I have been called to wear.

The hardships I faced during my upbringing were nothing short of a forecast, demonstrating how God would use these circumstances to refine me in a way that would make me pliable for His purpose. They kept me steady on a firm foundation so

I could assist others dealing with similar tribulations. He knew my heart sought how to fill a God-sized void in my directionless life. In what I believe was a moment of recalibration, I was called to wear my first life-changing garment.

I did not realize that wearing the uniform of the United States Coast Guard was the first outward expression of my inward desire to serve and be a part of something greater than myself. This regimented and secure new way of life seemed to fit me like a glove. I was forged into a warrior, which seemed to render the remnants of the past trauma dead and gone. I grew to be confident in who I was as a person, developing the intrinsic values of honor, respect, and devotion to duty instilled by serving. I learned what it meant to be selfless and the value of relational connection, but something was still missing. Then like an avalanche, one phone call changed the trajectory of my life.

THIS IS WHEN GOD CALLED ME TO PUT ON THE GARMENT OF SALVATION. THIS DECREE OF COVERING MEANT MY LIFE WAS NOW ONE OF DIGNITY, AUTHORITY, PROSPERITY AND PURITY, IN JESUS' NAME.

One of my shipmates was murdered while on leave. While death and loss are not unfamiliar territory in the Armed Forces, the loss of a shipmate is like losing a piece of your own soul. You are trained to completely depend on each other, to be a family, and support system. The tragedy of my friend's passing was bitterly felt.

This moment planted a deeply rooted seed of doubt, a seed that would sprout and wreak havoc on my life and faith in God. My feelings of safety and security, because I was in the military, were now traded in for fear and uncertainty. If death and pain could still touch me here, I would never be safe. I was consumed by the never-ending question: *Would I ever be able to feel whole again?*

On the way to the funeral, I grasped for a moment of peace. I tried to focus on the goodness of who my shipmate was, rather than the loss of his life. I decided to write to his mother.

I poured out every detail of the person I knew him to be on to the paper. That letter sparked a connection the Lord knew we both needed. My friend's mom showed me the love and grace of God in such tragedy. Her faith sparked a deep desire in me for divine connection. This is when God called me to put on the garment of Salvation. This decree of covering meant my life was now one of dignity, authority, prosperity, and purity, in Jesus' name.

In May of 2005, I dedicated my life to the Lord and was baptized, making this my second outward declaration of an inward change. Only this time, my service in the Coast Guard became a platform to share the richness of my divine connection with God instead where I placed all my hope. Being active duty provided a pathway to spiritual peace in a way I had never experienced. The more I served, the more I felt connected. What I did not realize was my engagement with God essentially became a transactional relationship.

I fell into the trap of believing if I was the dutiful daughter who did and said the "right things," then my heavenly Father would say "yes" to all of my demands.

In this portrait of perfection, it somehow helped me hide the lingering pain I hid behind the mask I wore so well. But I quickly found I was not in a position to bargain with God, and the pain grew harder to mask, despite my self-centered efforts.

Holding on to salvation like a contractual negotiation left me feeling angrier with myself, betrayed by God, and overwhelmed by what felt like relentless punishment. I could never seem to measure up. The more I clinched the trials and tribulations in my own strength, the more I dwindled away. My desperation for wholeness left me so broken, there was nothing left of myself to offer anyone else. I was stripped of everything the world told me I was—the hopes I had for myself and the blind illusion of control were taken away.

However, in this bare and vulnerable state, my heart was getting cleansed and purified. God was readying me for usefulness in His Kingdom purpose as His witness, not for my own vain, self-seeking desires. In this season of metamorphosis, God called me to wear the garment of faith.

For the first time, I was able to move beyond seeing God through the lens of my pain to seeing Him in the light of His true character and love for my heart. Surrender and salvation moved beyond contractual negotiation to a rich and true relational connection. I relinquished the internal struggle of needing to wear the mask of how I was "supposed" to be. I was no longer afraid to show Him the ugliness of my humanness. I finally conceded to His invitation and allowed every aspect of who I am in the darkest parts within me show, so His light could heal and restore all I'd lost.

Throughout the Bible, there are many references to a refinement process. Refining allows God to use our trials and tribulations to develop an authentic faith.

Scriptures also portray exchanging the clothing of this world for God's desire to cover us in His perfect design. We shed the rags of the past and are dressed in spiritual edification.

Growing our faith and understanding teaches us how to build a spiritual stance upon God's foundation of truth and righteousness—it's the only thing that can withstand the brokenness of this world. As our perspectives become more Christ-like, we grow in knowledge that the Lord does not take delight in the interim pressure of this world. Our eternal value is more about the strength of our character in Him than about the ease of our lives. The uniform of salvation and faith provide everything our hurting hearts need.

DANIELLE WHALEN is a self-proclaimed "King's Daughter" who loves the Lord, cherishes her family, and is passionate about uplifting others to know their true value in God! With over 15 years of professional experience in crisis intervention gained by serving as a Master's level clinical social worker, Coast Guard member, and ministry leader for Celebrate Recovery, Danielle is dedicated to bridging the disparities of mental health and spiritual wellness through writing, speaking, and Christian counseling. Her writing and speaking experience was developed early on through the U.S. Coast Guard as a trained team facilitator, senior mentor, and training coordinator for staff members. She is now dedicated to use these skills for exhortation and discipleship. To get connected with Danielle you can find more information at www.DanielleWhalen.org or on Facebook @DanielleWhalenWCC.

Chapter Thirty-Two
A LEGACY OF VALOR

MEGAN BROWN

I REMEMBER WHERE I was standing when the twin towers of the World Trade Center became the target of terrorists. It was 2001, I was a junior in high school, sixteen years young, and utterly grief-stricken. While standing in front of a vending machine, the simplicity that existed before I had dropped my quarters in for a snack vanished instantly. One of my classmates ran breathlessly down the broad hall toward me. Tears cascaded from his face. He stammered. "We. Are. Under attack." I didn't understand what he was talking about, though I would soon see the horrific act he was referencing unfold before my eyes.

I shuffled from the hall into a classroom. Everyone's eyes were fixed on the television set that had been rolled into the room. We watched the live events on the national news. Class instruction halted for the remainder of the day, as we huddled and hung on the video footage. The reporter's solemnness stung bitterly. Suddenly, the silence on the screen was broken by the sound of a plane crashing through the second tower. We erupted in screams.

My eyes darted around the room. I was desperately trying to gain control of my thoughts. *What is happening? Is this the end of the world?* My mind raced like this through the rest of the long school day.

When I finally bolted through the door of my house that afternoon, I immediately fell into my mother's arms. Traumatized by the whole experience, our family spent the rest of the evening glued to the news stations. We wept and spoke few words.

After 9/11, a wave of patriotism swept the nation. I had never seen a people so unified. Flags flew outside of nearly every home. Neighbors supported one another. Strangers shared embraces. Eventually, life progressed at a normal pace and I graduated in 2003. But even after school, the consequences and ripple effects of September 11, 2001 had not fully taken hold in my heart.

When I reflect on those years, I am freshly heartbroken at the extent of all I couldn't understand. I really didn't know exactly how much would change. Still today, after nearly fifteen years spent as a military spouse, the weight of loss and uncertainty still hangs heavy over me.

I was accepted to Louisiana State University at the Shreveport campus and I left for college—totally unprepared. Maybe because of immaturity or due to my complete lack of career path clarity, my collegiate interlude was brief. I found myself unable to find financial security and felt frustrated over the holding pattern that seemed to define my life. I longed to believe in something bigger than myself. Ultimately, I wandered into an Air Force recruiter's office.

One appointment was all it took, I signed a contract and enlisted into military service. I dreamed of laying the foundation I would build my new life upon. With a steady paycheck, I planned on saving and becoming responsible. I imagined the possibility of higher education without student debt. Simultaneously, I daydreamed about a future husband, and maybe even a family. The Air Force became my path for a fresh start.

> **I LONGED TO BELIEVE IN SOMETHING BIGGER THAN MYSELF.**

While in the early processes of enlistment, my motivation was obtaining security and total independence. I wanted to explore, travel, and kickstart my new life. I brimmed with excitement.

I scored well on the practice ASVAB—the Armed Service Vocational Aptitude Battery—a test that assesses a person's aptitude to determine active duty job placement. I discovered I was qualified to do most jobs in the Air Force. I passed all of my preliminary physicals, and then I jumped on a bus to MEPS—the Military Entrance Processing Station. At MEPS, men and women desiring to enter into military service are examined, processed, assigned a job, and swear into the Delayed Enlistment Program where they await their ship out date.

In preparation, I bought a new navy-blue suit with pinstripes. I pressed my shirt in the early hours at the hotel across from the processing center. I could hardly sleep because of the anticipation.

Crisp and clean in my new power suit, I stormed the doors to take the official test, pass a physical, be assigned a job, and take an oath of service. When my test was completed, my physical conducted, and with a clenched job in contracting in hand, it was time to "swear in."

If I close my eyes, I can still picture the MEPS Ceremony Room. I was surrounded by my peers—men and women who shared the love of our country and fundamentally believed in the ideals of service before self. In the very front of the group, standing resolute before the flag, I raised my right hand and swore the oath. "I, Megan Buehring, do solemnly swear that I will support and defend the Constitution of the United States against all enemies, foreign and domestic; that I will bear true faith and allegiance to the same; and that I will obey the orders of the President of the United States and the orders of the officers appointed over me, according to the regulations and the Uniform Code of Military Justice. So help me God."

In that moment, my paradigm shifted. No longer was my draw to military service one of stability, but a response to the call of sacrifice—the loud and resounding call to valor. Something inside me changed forever, and I can't go back.

During my time awaiting a "ship out" date, I caught a glimpse of a stunningly handsome man in an Air Force blues uniform. Instantly, I was charmed. I won't say it was "love at first sight," but I would be lying if I didn't say the feelings were immense and unbelievably swift. After a few meals together, Keith (now my husband of nearly fifteen years), decided this was "it." Faced with the possibility of a long-term separation, he came up with an alternate plan—a proposal.

Six short weeks later, we were wed in a small church in Columbus, MS. My dreams of a future had come true. The boundless time I had spent conjuring up the perfect life met its demise at the end of an altar. There he stood, a loving and kind man of God, with his eyes firmly fixed on mine. The Air Force no longer represented my door of opportunity, granting my freedom. Instead, it was a man in fierce pursuit of God that would bring about my liberation.

Eventually, my new husband led me to the Lord. Keith's selflessness, patience, and discipling began to shape me into the woman I am today. As I look back, I can see God's handwriting in the DNA of our relationship. I can see Him working in and through every seemingly strange coincidence. God had always known I would serve Him, even if it was not in the way I planned. Stepping away from my enlistment contract allowed me to answer a different call toward valor—wifedom and motherhood.

Every once in a while, there is a stirring in my heart. I long to share a connection with the vibrant women who wear the uniform. I hold and respect their deeply embodied beliefs of duty, honor, and integrity. They are warriors, and maybe one day I'll join their ranks.

For now, I will continue walking on the path the Lord has designed for me as a wife to an American airman, a mom to four high-energy kids, and as a servant to His people. I thought I had my life mapped out. However, I learned that God's plan is always better than our own.

MEGAN BROWN is a seasoned military spouse and military missionary. She is the Military Liaison for the Speak Up Conference Global Missions Military Scholarship and the 2019-Armed Forces Insurance Robins AFB Military Spouse of the Year. She is passionate about military mission work, teaching, and preaching about Jesus in and out of the local church. Her Bible study, "Esther: Come Out of Hiding," published by Moody Publishers in Chicago, will release in April 2021. She lives in middle Georgia with her husband, Keith, and their energetic kiddos. She is a Bible teacher, speaker, and freelance writer. To learn more or connect with Megan, visit www.meganbbrown.com.

Chapter Thirty-Three
WARRIOR WITHIN — LEADING MYSELF

SHERRY EIFLER

BEAT YOUR FACE!" the Drill Sergeant yelled at Private Lowe, just a few feet away from me. She began to beat her cheeks with her hands rapidly. Drill Sergeant's firm response was, "Push-ups! That is what 'beat your face' means. Now give me ten!"

Welcome to Army Basic Training, my summer vacation from college. It was there I learned that battle-buddies are life-savers, officers are to be feared, and "gas" isn't just for cars. Basic training began to awaken the warrior within me.

I quickly transformed from a Specialist in the Army Reserve to a Cadet in the Reserve Officer Training Corps (ROTC). My fear of officers softened into admiration. It awakened my drive to become an officer who would be respected, not feared.

ROTC is where I found my people and my purpose—leadership in community.

I realize now that the seemingly natural choices I made were providential. Being commissioned as an Army Officer started a crescendo of activity over the next twenty months. I got engaged, became a new Army wife, and became the first college graduate in my family. Before I could catch my breath, I was sent to the Medical Service Officer Basic Course.

Home became wherever the Army took my husband and me. Our first two years of marriage resulted in only seven months of living in the same house and sleeping in the same bed. We were both on the fast track, having been selected for next level assignments and finding our niche. However, I was conflicted with how to balance my dual role as both an Army officer and an Army wife.

My commander instilled in me that leadership is about people, not just accomplishments. In the middle of my Emergency Medical Technician training, I planned part of our Field Training Exercise, which was the turning point for my Ambulance Platoon. My platoon developed a newfound respect for their "butter bar" Lieutenant. We all developed a team mindset.

Military marriage also requires a team mindset, especially when both are soldiers. Sacrifice is woven into the cloth the spouses wear. When called to sacrifice, neither hesitates, for they know the cost is worth their love. Sacrifice was required as my Airborne Ranger was selected for his dream job, which meant he would move. "Go, baby, go!" my heart and words shouted, even as my mind screamed, *No! My dream job is here!*

He moved. I wrapped up my job and put my dream on the shelf. Leaders sacrifice.

The beginning of the end of my active duty service soon followed. I arrived at our new location, determined to make peace with the knowledge that I had sacrificed my previous dream. I put my marriage first, with new hope that I might realize my dream in our new location. Surprisingly, that hope was shot down quickly. This unknown Lieutenant wasn't getting considered for a career progressing job.

I spent the next two years learning to lead myself. To lead through discouraging assignments, dismissed sexual harassment, my husband's deployment, and marital challenges, all while gleaning from the leaders around me. Leading myself meant recognizing when it was time to say goodbye.

Soon, I realized my purpose was no longer serving, but rather to support those who served. I humbly transitioned from Army Captain Eifler to Inactive Army Reserve Captain Eifler.

When my transition was official, I was filled with emotion. *Is this really what I want? What have I done?*

Hesitantly, I traded my Active Duty Identification (ID) card for a Dependent ID card. I was bombarded by lingering "what if" thoughts. A familiar enemy was trying to prevent me from moving forward with confidence. I mentally fought back. *Defeat the enemy of doubt, Warrior! Lob your grenade on the "what if" bunker and move out smartly!*

Grenade launched, I found confidence as I reminded myself that my heart's desire was to be a devoted mother and Army wife. A quiet sense of strength came over me again. I knew I would lead myself through this transition and come out stronger on the other side. In order to begin, I had to learn to be led by the Leader of all leaders—Jesus Christ, now the Lord of my life.

We eventually became parents. From the start, we were quickly stripped of the joy of exploring all the firsts together. Daddy would be in Korea near the demilitarized zone in just one month, while Mommy and baby lived in Michigan. My impulse was to grab control of what I could, and to hold on tightly to my control each day.

Back home, my dad's guiding voice called me to church. Ultimately, I surrendered my control and trusted my life and will to Jesus. He was the answer to my identity crisis, a crisis so many military spouses are challenged with, when they must step away from a career and into a dependent role. Or when motherhood or some other heightened responsibility requires focus.

Those two years apart made my husband and me stronger in Christ, ready to step confidently into our tomorrows. When we were together again, we grew in our leadership, spiritual understanding, friendships, and family size.

LOOKING BACK, I CAN SEE THE POWER OF RELEASE.

While moving again, I received calls from Army Reserve units asking about my interest in activating and serving in their unit. I began to consider if maybe this would be a good time to slip back into uniform. An unexpected, official letter arrived. It forced me to make a serious decision. *Should I continue as an Army Reserve Officer or resign my commission?*

As I looked across the room at our then six-month-old, twenty-one-month-old, and four-year-old, I realized it was time to completely surrender the soldier part of my identity and trust that I was enough in Christ. If another war happened, Brian would soldier on, my place would be at home. With confidence and peace, I signed the resignation paperwork in July 2001. Just two months later, our country was attacked. We all remember where we were that Tuesday morning, on September 11, 2001.

9/11 was the day the Lord began dusting off the dream I had put on the shelf, preparing me to see it through His eyes—even as He prepared me for so much more. As I stepped into my new role as a professional volunteer, making a difference for both soldiers and their families, I knew it wouldn't be long before my purpose of leadership in the community activated. My experience as both a soldier and spouse equipped me for that role.

Looking back, I can see the power of release. My obedience to sacrifice and surrender my dream opened my heart to receive and live out God's desires, what He placed in my heart. He was able to accomplish so much more eternal value through His warrior princess, when she worked alongside those who serve. My life proves we can trust God's requests.

So, let me ask you. What dreams have you put on the shelf? How many times have you questioned *What if?* or *If only?*

If we are willing to dust off the dreams we've shelved *and* place them in the Lord's hands, we will see He has so much more for us than we ever imagine achieving. For me, the warrior within seemed to have been put on a shelf when my dream to serve as a commander was left to collect dust. But the Lord was stirring His warrior spirit in me, preparing me for the moment I would step into my full identity found in Him.

In the waiting, we must avoid the "what if" minefields and remember—surrender and sacrifice are the call. We lead ourselves when we place our hopes in the hands of the Dream Creator. He will revitalize our dreams if we will dust them off and place them in His hands.

(See Sherry Eifler's bio in Chapter Twelve)

Chapter Thirty-Four
A CALL TO STEP BOLDLY

―――

RICHELLE FUTCH

I JOINED THE MILITARY at eighteen for salvation. I remember listening to Journey's, *Don't Stop Believin'* and fantasizing about a life beyond the circumstances I was living in. I imagined hopping on a train to anywhere and escaping the small-town prison I felt was restricting me.

My parents had separated when I was sixteen, and they both struggled with making decisions for their new lives, which left me behind. They both moved out, and I lived in a house my grandma owned, with my older brother.

For the next two years, my life was uncertain. I graduated high school, ended an abusive relationship, slept in my car sometimes, or crashed at friends' houses. Yet I always kept an "I'm fine" attitude. I truly believed I needed to slowly keep doing one thing that would grow me in some way.

I used financial aid to go to community college. I worked

at a restaurant and a work study job at the college, all the while thinking, *I'm stepping slowly in the right direction. But I need to leap. I need one big leap forward, so I can feel like I am getting somewhere.* This belief in myself was strong, and yet I lacked the opportunity or adult guidance to create a different life for myself.

I remember thinking how attractive the military appeared, as it meant having a job, a place to live, food, and money for college. At eighteen, it was everything I needed in one easy signature. Living for a few years in uncertainty and in an abusive relationship made it easy for me to overlook the safety aspect of the decision. I leaned into this wonderful opportunity the military offered me to make it on my own. I remember telling myself: *You aren't running from something—you are running to something.*

My first time going anywhere alone, I boarded a plane to Parris Island, South Carolina for Marine Corps bootcamp. I sat in the reception line with the other recruits and smiled. I was so happy to be anywhere but home. Other girls looked scared, most had their heads down, some were crying, but I kept my chin raised.

Through basic training, it was very similar, lots of girls cried, while I smiled. I was meritoriously promoted out of bootcamp for finishing at the top of my platoon. Things were great, until they weren't.

One of the things often overlooked, when it comes to the military members and their spouses as a whole, is what we bring into the service. What do we carry in with us that impacts our views and abilities to navigate stressful times?

Once again, I attracted an abusive partner. I suffered trauma inside the military. I approached my service much like I did my life back home—privately and alone. I believed that choosing to suffer, if it gained me other favors, was acceptable and sometimes necessary. And during my time in the service, I was not deepening my understanding of faith in God. I usually prayed at night before bed (and sometimes not even that), but this was all I offered in the way of my relationship with God. I relied on the bottle more than anything.

My behavior changed a lot when I was drinking. I had zero regard for my own life. I struggled with suicidal thoughts under the influence. I became reckless. I did not really want to take my own life, but if I died doing something extreme, so be it. I justified playing hard in my own mind, reminding myself how functioning and successful I was.

While taking a college speech class, I was asked to give an introduction on who you are and where you plan to be in three, five, and ten years. I remember confidently delivering the "I don't plan to be alive at 30" line. The faces in the room stared back at me. At twenty-one years old, thirty seemed so far away. I really didn't see a future for myself. It wasn't that I didn't see it, I just didn't care about it. Experiencing trauma felt like that for me.

It is really easy to go unnoticed in the military. Actually, it is really easy to go unnoticed in the world in general. You can feel dark feelings and still function around other people—I felt that way for years.

I didn't *stay* in the dark, however. I started operating in a different way. I began contributing to causes and people that fueled my passions. When I got out of the military and pursued my undergraduate degree, I started volunteering as a Court Appointed Special Advocate (CASA). I represented a voice for children who were placed in foster care in the courts. Speaking up for those who could not speak for themselves gave me purpose. If I didn't care about my future, I certainly could show up for *them*. That got me through for a while.

Then after I graduated, I started working as a counselor at a boys' prison. The main treatment we used for counseling was a therapy called Dialectical Behavior Therapy. In order for me to be the best at my job, I found I needed to apply the teachings to my own life, so I could explain and teach them to others. This got me to a place where I began to identify my unhealthy patterns. It was more than just recognizing the problems—it was doing new things in place of the problems. All of a sudden, life just got easier.

I wish I could tell you there was some special program in the military that changed my life. I wish I could say there was this one person in my chain of command who saw something, pulled me aside, and offered advice and support. The fact is, that never happened for me. The only consistent relationship I ever had was my relationship with God.

THE ONLY CONSISTENT RELATIONSHIP I EVER HAD, WAS MY RELATIONSHIP WITH GOD.

Through all of it, He never wavered. I used to believe that following Christ was easier when things were good. When I was overwhelmed, and the weight of my problems were heavy, I wouldn't think of unloading my concerns on Him. But now I feel the opposite. He is the first place I go to unload.

Today, my life is very different. I am a mental health counselor and a military spouse. My work is focused around advocating for military families to reduce stress and avoid suicide, using the same skills that helped me. I teach workshops around military installations in the U.S. and abroad. I feel called to be a light for others through their dark times. I'm reminded of 1 Peter 5: 1-11.

> *To the Elders and the Flock*
> *To the elders among you, I appeal as a fellow elder and a witness of Christ's sufferings who also will share in the glory to be revealed: Be shepherds of God's*

flock that is under your care, watching over them— not because you must, but because you are willing, as God wants you to be; not pursuing dishonest gain, but eager to serve; not lording it over those entrusted to you, but being examples to the flock. And when the Chief Shepherd appears, you will receive the crown of glory that will never fade away.

In the same way, you who are younger, submit yourselves to your elders. All of you, clothe yourselves with humility toward one another, because,

"God opposes the proud but shows favor to the humble."

Humble yourselves, therefore, under God's mighty hand, that he may lift you up in due time. Cast all your anxiety on him because he cares for you.

Be alert and of sober mind. Your enemy the devil prowls around like a roaring lion looking for someone to devour. Resist him, standing firm in the faith, because you know that the family of believers throughout the world is undergoing the same kind of sufferings.

And the God of all grace, who called you to his eternal glory in Christ, after you have suffered a little while, will himself restore you and make you strong, firm and steadfast. To him be the power for ever and ever. Amen. (1 Peter 5:1-11 NIV)

This is how I envision our military community. This is how I envision our civilian community.

Like I did as a CASA, speaking up for children who did not yet have a voice, I speak up for those who are too tired to speak. I represent those too emotional to find the words, or for whatever reason, who just need someone to start the conversation. Then, I help them gain the skills to speak up for themselves.

I am willing and eager to serve. I've lost too many friends to suicide or drug overdoses to stay silent. My past experiences led to my present purpose.

Believing in God is not the same as having faith in God. I understand the difference now, and that has made all the difference in my life. It allows me to find meaning and understanding in temporary disappointments and glory in my blessings.

If you feel like I did for many years, alone, surrounded by people, I assure you, through Christ you are never alone. He is the way. Counseling helps. Contributing helps. However, without belief and faith in something bigger than yourself, the dark days will stay dark and the loneliness will continue creeping back. Every day you wake up with a choice—stay in the dark, or step boldly into the light.

RICHELLE is a Marine Corps Veteran and Military Spouse to an Army Special Forces Non-Commissioned Officer. She has over 15 years of clinical experience working with government agencies, as well as in private practice. She received her Master's in Social Work from the University of Washington, has worked in the juvenile justice system, and counseled Soldiers and their families in the Warrior Transition Battalion. With extensive training in Dialectical Behavior Therapy (DBT), Richelle has generalized DBT skills to various populations. She is passionate about addressing stress in military families to help reduce suicide.

This passion lead to the development of her workshop, Unpacking Your Emotional Ruck, and her book *Her Ruck: Inside the Emotional Backpack of Military Wives*, which has provided opportunities to serve military families worldwide. She is a member of the directorate team of Military Spouse Behavioral Health Clinicians and key advisor of the Military Special Operations Family Collaborative. Richelle was recently awarded Armed Forces Insurance Fort Bragg Military Spouse of the Year for 2019, recognized for her professional impact as well as extensive volunteer service within our military community. Learn more about Richelle or follow her work at Richellefutch.com

Epilogue
THE WARRIOR ARCHETYPE

DANIELLE WHALEN

WOMEN OF THE military are cut from a different cloth in many ways because of the extraordinary experiences and obstacles which have shaped who they are. Being a military woman goes beyond the uniform she or her loved one wears, it is a garment worn at the depths of who she is. Once she puts it on, the civilian world never fits quite the same way again.

This unique sisterhood is comprised of the mothers, sisters, daughters, wives, and service women of our armed forces. The value of her instinctual nurturing, coupled with the enduring strength of carrying the weight of world peace on her shoulders, is both a blessing and her deepest vulnerability. However, this well of vulnerability is where she can draw her greatest strength from. It is in this place where a woman is transformed into a warrior through awareness of her pain and sacrifice. But, fearless in the face of uncertainty, she pushes beyond herself with perseverance and courage.

The very essence of a military woman is the embodiment of the warrior archetype. These women stand as our modern-day heroes, but do we consider what is at their core being? With a guarded heart, her mission comes from the inside out. What is not seen is her broken heart from countless sleepless nights of worry. The hardest days, when getting out of bed seems impossible, take place behind closed doors. The gaping hole of loss, the battle of lies in her head that tell her she is worthless, the loneliness of constant moving and change, feelings of isolation, and a fear that threatens to paralyze haunt her daily thoughts. In the suffering others don't see, she transforms it into a purpose that drives her forward.

This woman is the same mother who is proud of her child's service, but fears the heartbreaking knock on the door. She's the sister who misses her best friend. She's the daughter who prays every night for her parent's safe return. She's the wife who wears the brave face, while trying to keep the family together—she pushes aside her fears of the unknown. She's the service woman who puts everything on the line in sacrifice for her country, only to return home to find a world that is forced to move on without her—demanding her to try and catch up. Each of these women, with a deep longing for what is relinquished, but a bitter understanding for the greater need of those sacrifices, gives her all for others.

Stripped down and heavy burdened are the shoulders of the military woman who offers only her authentic self. The hand that will feed the hungry, the heart that will grieve with her sisters, the words that demand change in injustice, faith that will move a mountain, and a mind of victory over any obstacle that may lay upon her path—this is she. Even in moments where she feels the remnants of herself are tattered from the long road of adversity, she continues—one step after the next. Each time trumpets of distress are sounded, she fortifies herself, and runs toward the call of consoling the world around her.

As she presses into the pain, the warrior woman knows she is not alone in her mission, and with that sweet surrender, the sense of community emerges. So, she picks herself back up, dries her eyes, and continues marching to the mantra of, "If I can do just one thing to make a difference for someone like me, it is worth it." This will eternally be her wellspring of empowerment.

Always keeping one foot in the source of her vulnerability, and the other navigating a continuous alignment with what is important to her, she forges on. The capacity to give unwavering love in the face of many unseen battles is the cornerstone of these warrior women.

A WARRIOR WOMAN'S STRENGTH OF MIND COMES ONLY FROM A BELIEF BEYOND SELF.

A warrior woman's strength of mind comes only from a belief beyond self. They are leaders among servants who are called upon to be world changers, but they are often left without the resources to replenish all they give away. When you look to one of these women, who exude strength and courage, know that her selflessness of service comes at a premium cost, a relentless act of giving every single piece of her heart.

My aim in sharing the warrior archetype is to challenge our society in the way we support and engage our military community. Too often and easily, they are taken for granted. The level of excellence poured out from our military counterparts is mostly overlooked and disregarded. With little afterthought, we take what warrior women are willing to give up and forget it comes at a deep cost. We say thank you, and we are appreciative of those forfeitures, but we neglect to search deeper for the human behind those sacrifices. We fail to show reciprocity, because we do not consider key questions that would provide insight.

"How has service impacted you?" we should ask. We make choices about how the military will serve our country, but we turn a blind eye when the consequences of those choices are too unbearable and uncomfortable to watch.

"Has anyone told you how much you, and what you give, are appreciated?" we should say. Simple acknowledgement is a powerful force.

"Is there anything I can do to support you?" we should offer. Leaving our warriors to carry the weight and sacrifices alone must come to an end. It is imperative that we start asking the hard questions of how serving is impacting the people around us and provide meaningful ways to stand alongside them.

We can no longer remain satisfied with a bystander approach as people suffer in silence, while trying to forge forward. Humanity must be the highest component of community in order to offer the kind of restoration and recovery that our warrior women often need.

To the warrior archetype, my greatest gratitude is offered to you for your sacrifice in service to our country. The many thankless acts and love you so selflessly give of yourself truly make a difference in this world! The days are long, and the years are short my friend, but know we are blessed you are a part of them. Whether you are charging forward stronger than ever, or need to brush your knees off and start over, I offer my hand to you, Sister. Know I'm on your side—in your darkest despair or on the brightest of days.

I hope to ignite discussion in your honor that will encourage ownership and responsibility in caring for one another. We *are* our sister's keepers. To move beyond words of support, but to take them into action, is what it means to truly stand in the gap for one another. My heart and prayers are with you.